THE DUNG BEETLE BEETLE MANAGER

Harry,

Keep Rolling the
Raw material and
making great PMs.
Thanks for a great
YDI experience,

Scott

THE DUNG BEETLE MANAGER

SCOTT W. DUNLAP

Outskirts Press, Inc.
Denver, Colorado

The Dung Beetle Manager
All Rights Reserved.
Copyright © 2009 Scott W. Dunlap
v3.0

Cover Photo © 2009 JupiterImages Corporation. All rights reserved - used with permission.

Outskirts Press, Inc.
http://www.outskirtspress.com

ISBN: 978-1-4327-4416-8

Library of Congress Control Number: 2009932955

Outskirts Press and the "OP" logo are trademarks belonging to Outskirts Press, Inc.

PRINTED IN THE UNITED STATES OF AMERICA

DEDICATION

This book is dedicated to my wife, Robin, my daughters, Britt and Laura, and my grandsons, David Scott and Keelan. To Robin, we're still here after all these years even when I haven't been. That says a lot about your love and commitment to me and holding our family together regardless of storms we have faced. And you are still the record holder in my federal experience for successfully holding government personnel accountable and actually firing them when needed. To Britt and Laura, you have both grown into beautiful young women and I am very proud of you. To my mom and family back in Arkansas, you gave me these roots so you still have to claim me. And to the man who had me believing my name was "Dumbass" most of my teen years, my beloved dad, Bill Dunlap, may you rest in God's eternal peace.

To the men, women, and families of our armed forces, you are our reason to go to work and dive into the pile every day, God bless you all for your service. And lastly, to all my friends and colleagues who over time have both inspired and exhausted me in our quest for the next dung ball. It has been a privilege to serve our country with you.

TABLE OF CONTENTS

CHAPTER 1

THE POOSPIRATION

It all started a long time ago, back in farm country in Walnut Ridge, Arkansas. My dad, brother, and I would munch down on Mom's staples of the South – brown beans, cornbread, and fresh green onions right out of the garden. Forty minutes later, we would be shooed out of the house to go fart on the lawn. The upside to our gas parties was that mosquitoes (the state bird in Arkansas) were less likely to bother us. It was sort of like having a redneck citronella candle emanating out of your butt. But that is not the real inspiration for this book, just a homey remembrance of quieter and more laid back times.

I have to get this out there right up front. Farts are funny, everybody shits, shit stinks, and shit happens. Now get over your squeamishness about the idea of using shit and dung beetles as metaphors for higher learning in the ways of organizational dynamics and human behavior. I won't continue using the word "shit" too much, rather opting for something more sensible to the snooty or highbrow reader. I struggled with the best shit replacement term because there are so many – poo, dung, scat, turd, feces, droppings, excrement, and crap, to name a few. Shit's shit, folks – plain and simple. Yours doesn't stink as bad as someone else's, but sometimes you score a real ten that is eye-watering even to yourself. So we'll go with dung pat, poo, scat, or turd as the socially acceptable terms for the remainder of this book. Well, at least some of the time.

Now back to the inspiration. Aside from sitting in the yard having fart fights with my dad and brother, I really did have a few butt-scratching moments of learning from my youth. The great Yogi Berra was quoted as saying, "You can observe a lot just by watching." Sir Isaac Newton was chilling under an apple tree and discovered the force of gravity by observing an apple fall to the ground. One day when I was shoveling cow manure for my uncle, I observed a lone beetle quietly working his way out of a steamy mass of a cow patty. I found it both fascinating and disgusting that this bug was burrowing out of fresh cow manure. The escape from Pooville was bad enough, but as he emerged, I could see the form of a finely shaped ball. Shortly after he emerged from the pile with his nice round ball, the beetle population increased and it looked like they were fighting over the turd ball old Stinky had just rolled. This behavior was curious, fascinating, and way more relevant to your day job than you might imagine.

Have you ever wondered about the origin of the term "shit"? The earliest origins of the term "scittan," "scitta," "schete," and "schite" all relate to cattle with diarrhea, excrement, or contemptible people. And so it went, with the word "shit" evolving to become the centerpiece of folksy communications everywhere. "Shit hot," "ain't that some shit," "shit happens," "no shit," "you're shitting me," "when the shit hits the fan," "up shit creek," "holy shit," "oh shit," "shit ass," "shit head," "shit for brains," "full of shit," "bullshit," and my favorite – the two syllable version of shit that is used in the Deep South – "she-yut." By the way, I knew I had evolved to a higher level of literacy when I left Arkansas and discovered that "shit" is actually a single-syllable word. That was a big day for me. If the Department of Defense had discovered shit, I am convinced the name would have been an acronym for something denoting death and destruction, like "Sub-rectal High-Intensity Turd."

Speaking of shit, death, and destruction, gunpowder requires an ingredient of potassium nitrate, also known as "saltpeter." During the early 1700s and before, the primary source of saltpeter was via organic animal refuse, otherwise known as poop. Poop collectors would go out and collect the raw material to stock up for making gun powder. During the 1800s, people would enter into contracts to sell their outhouse deposits that included niter, or saltpeter, to the government. And you thought recycling was a trendy twentieth-century thing. If there had been a Pentagon (five sided tent) in the early days, I'm sure there would have been a Department of Dung that was responsible for finding and stockpiling the poo. Being the latrine officer in those days would have been a very prestigious job. In modern times, people are still selling their crap to the government, but the outhouse has been replaced with lobbyists and retired government officials helping to perpetuate the species.

The term "bullshit" has a special place in my heart and on the job. Metaphorically speaking, bullshit (as opposed to heifer shit, which actually looks the same) is a big pile of crap and it stinks. I don't know anyone who hasn't said "bullshit" at least once in their life. The fact that people say it so often validates my premise that there is more to be learned from observing those who drop it and those responsible for cleaning it up than you might imagine. The only way there could be no bullshit in the workforce is if there were no humans in the workforce. It is interesting that the term "bullshit" does not always mean the facts are bad. I have seen rock-solid truth referred to as bullshit by those who did not wish to see the truth, and did not like what the facts were telling them. All bullshit is not the same. It is in the eye and nose of the beholder.

The military has a saying for "the situation is bad, so live with it." The saying is "embrace the suck." After joining the navy, going to college, getting a graduate degree, working in a regional bank, getting a job with the federal government, and embracing the "bureaucratic suck" while observing the dynamics of the workforce and geopolitical machine in action for about twenty years, that little turd-rolling bug came back to mind. The association began forming for me when one of my favorite colleagues named Pat rewarded me with a small owl pellet in a pill bottle. Pat is special in a lot of ways, and it is still hard for me to understand how she ended up working for the federal government. Her first husband was a part of Frank Zappa's band, so she was exposed to a different kind of brilliance early in her life. To understand her influences, you need to get your head around a couple of Frank Zappa's notable quotes:

- "Some scientists claim that hydrogen, because it is so plentiful, is the basic building block of the universe. I dispute that. I say there is more stupidity than hydrogen, and that is the basic building block of the universe."
- "Without deviation from the norm, 'progress' is not possible."
- "Politics is the entertainment branch of industry."
- "May your shit come to life and kiss you on the face."

If you could appreciate Pat's intellect and sense of humor, you would work very effectively with her. Pat had a theory that if you did not appreciate the writings of Douglas Adams, you would not likely see the bureaucratic pink elephant in the room that was usually camped out in every meeting. Pat used a fuse analogy to assess the mental processing lead time from presentation of obvious fact to action. There were four types of fuses: normal, premature, delayed, and duds. Normally fused bureaucrats (who understood *The Hitchhiker's Guide to the Galaxy*) would generally make a balanced conclusion concurrent with hearing the facts.

Prematurely fused bureaucrats would jump to conclusions long before the facts were presented or complete. Delay fused bureaucrats would take days and weeks for the lights to come on. The duds, well, they just never got the point. She'd get the point and conclusions very quickly, and then get entertained watching most of the rest of the gang evolving through a bureaucratically induced haze to a profound grasp of the obvious. Almost like magic, it would be like someone flipped on the power switch, and the clueless came to their senses with the same realization she'd had days and weeks earlier. Either that or the big pink elephant in the room would just say "boo" or get into a brawl with the 800-pound gorilla sitting on his back.

For the uninformed, an owl pellet is an owl "pre-turd." I call it a pre-turd since it is the indigestible stuff like bones and feathers that owls puke up. If it had stuck around long enough in the owl's digestive system, it would have been an owl turd. Pat had been given the "award" when she worked with the Social Security Administration by a Native American senior executive. He told her it was symbolic of all the hard work she had done. As she had walked the streets of Harlem trying to change the world, she had reached out to many in need and was both touched and dismayed at the human condition. In the course of doing the hard work of being a civil servant in Harlem, she had experienced the best and worst of humanity. In the spirit of the owl, she had taken in the nourishing and sustaining parts of her job and people she served, and had to puke up the parts that did not settle well with her conscience in order to go back on the street the next day. Just as the wise owl ate to live, and barfed up the indigestible stuff, tribal wisdom would argue that she had achieved oneness with Mother Earth. She would have rather had a $500 cash award, but the owl pellet was one of the most unique management recognition tools she had ever come across in her career. After working with Pat for a couple of years and just before her retirement, she said she had observed in me the same qualities as the executive who gave her the owl pellet. Pat awarded me the owl pellet in the pill bottle and said with some confidence that it had found its true home. No truer words were ever spoken, and the owl pellet in a pill bottle remains on my desk to this day.

The final straw in the inspiration chain came to me one evening several years ago when I was watching a television documentary that featured dung beetles and other creatures that use feces as a source of life or a weapon. I performed a bit of research on the scarab beetle, otherwise known as the dung beetle. What an amazing little creature with quite a history. The dung beetle was worshipped by ancient Egyptians who believed that the dung beetles kept the earth turning either by rolling it under their feet or by rolling the sun across the sky. The beetle inspired their god Khepri, an enormous scarab who pushed the sun across the sky. That sort of makes sense if you have ever seen a dung beetle rolling a ball of poo, but most people would not immediately make that association. The African dung beetle is a distinguished poo-eater that uses moonlight to navigate into dung pats and avoids the competition for the tasty ball. They are stealthy and get in and out of the pile using the cover of darkness with moonlight to navigate by. Cave-dwelling dung beetles are blessed with mountains of bat and bird guano, and their continuous feasting actually keeps the smell down. There are three main types of dung beetles – rollers, tunnelers, and dwellers.

Rollers dig into the dung pat and roll up a neat ball, find a mate, then roll off to procreate, using the ball as both a source of nourishment and the host for their eggs. Imagine meeting your mate in a dung pat. How would you ever pick one out when they all look and smell the same? But that is another question for another time and book. As soon as rollers clear the dung pat, there is an onslaught of lazy, do-nothing, sideline-loving shit-eaters who attack and try to take the ball away. Don't get ahead of yourself here; the lazy, sideline-loving shit-eaters are just as essential to the ecosystem as the rollers. They just really piss you off.

Tunnelers take a more strategic route to their dinner (or nesting place) by digging a tunnel underneath the dung pat and up into it. Tunnelers avoid the conflict that often occurs when rollers try to leave the dung pat and other dung beetles try to steal the ball. Tunnelers are crafty, strategic, and end up having to work a lot harder digging through dirt instead of poo in order to get the job done. A lot of the engineers I have worked with over time are tunnelers because they take the more conservative, proven, and often longer routes to the outcome, but they usually get the job done well if you have the time and money.

Dwellers do just that. They live in the dung pat. Imagine living in an edible poo home that also serves as a nutrient-rich landscape for raising children. OK, not. Dwellers invariably have a hard time distinguishing between scat and anything else because they are always in it. They are very comfortable in their crappy circumstances and crappy job because they simply do not know any other way of living. There is great comfort in the familiar pile of shit. If you have ever had any kind of management training, I'm sure you heard the story of the frog in the water. If you put a frog in a pot of water at room temperature, then put a fire under the pot, the frog will not try to escape since the changes in water temperature are so gradual, and it will simply boil to death. However, if you try and toss the frog into that same pot of boiling water, he will raise hell trying to get out of the hot water. Dwellers are a lot like the frogs in the room temperature pots. Dwellers make change really, really difficult. The benefit from dwellers is that they represent the majority of the workforce, provide stability, and plod on regardless of the circumstances and scat tossed their way.

I'll spend more time describing the attributes and behaviors of our beetle types, but you get the picture. Poo, dung, feces, excrement, crap, shit – whatever it's called, it happens. We all do it, and some do it bigger and nastier than others. These people are called "executives." Then there are those who are forced to eat it, clean it, step in it, or get it thrown in their face. Those people are called "the workforce." Then there are the poor schmucks in the middle. These people are called "managers." This book is about them, the persistent Dung Beetle managers. Over the course of my career, I have watched and learned a lot from Dung Beetle managers. They dive into elephant droppings, try to make something useful out of it, only to find dozens of other dung beetles trying to take away their work. Some poo makes things grow, other poo is simply a stinky mess that just has to be cleaned up.

This book will talk about the various kinds of poo makers and those who clean it up. In the end, you will find great wisdom and insight from the Dung Beetle style of managing. And when you do, stand proud with the rest of the Beetles and say, "Roll on, dung beetles, roll on."

CHAPTER 2

SHIT'S FUNNY

I could not write this book without telling you a good shit story. Even better, a good all-American high school football shit story. I played football in a small double-A school in Arkansas with most of my childhood friends. To put this in perspective, you could have placed most of our entire senior class in a large oak tree for the class picture. My coach said I was the meanest, hardest-hitting 128-pounder they had on the team. You may not be impressed by the coach's compliment, but I was. That is why I was on the scrub team playing football on this particular Thursday night on a cool October evening in 1977.

What our scrub team lacked in skill, they made up in personality and style. On the line, we had such legendary players as "Buffalo Butt" and "Goober." Buffalo Butt was the left guard, and his claim to fame was mooning the cars following our player bus and unraveling rolls of toilet paper from the window. Not surprisingly, Buffalo Butt had a very big ass. One night during one of Buffalo Butt's moon fest, the car right behind the bus was being driven by the coach and his wife. Coach had no problem recognizing Buffalo Butt's ass the next day since it was by far the widest around. Also didn't help old Buffalo Butt that he would flip off cars following the bus and press his lips against the glass and puff up his face while doing so.

Goober, also known as "Goob," was the center. Goob was tall, lanky, and the consummate nerd who wanted to be a badass. Goob had a huge heart and extraordinary fight in him. His life story is more extraordinary than the one I will tell, but on this October evening, he redefined the delay of game penalty and the history of 2A high school Thursday night wanna-be football.

Roger was my best friend in high school, and we still keep in touch to this day. He was also the quarterback who had dreams of becoming a medical doctor as a very young man. Roger was never quite into the standard irresponsible teenage behaviors that could someday prevent him from being a doctor. He told me of his dream to be a doctor when I first met him and he never faltered in that goal. Through his association with me, it is nothing short of an act of God that he is in fact, today, a successful plastic surgeon in Arkansas.

Roger could throw a pass almost 60 yards standing with both feet firmly planted in place, and if he had protection he was lethal with his arm. I met Roger when he transferred to our school during our freshman year. I had just left the watermelon patch covered in dry, rotten watermelon innards, dirt, and sweat. I probably looked even worse than I smelled. Roger was very clean and did not stink. He said "hi," and I knew any new guy who could get past my watermelon funk and still be polite had to be quite a guy. He also drove a bi-centennial "Spirit of '76" red, white, and blue Chevy Vega, so you had to love the guy. During our high school days, Roger and I both were duly rejected by girls who would not ride in our un-cool automobiles. Roger's '76 Chevy Vega was an all-American machine. My gold 1968 Ford Ranger was a short wheel base pickup, three on the tree (that's a three-speed manual transmission with the shifter on the steering column for the non-gear head) with L-60's (really wide tires) and chrome rims in the back, chrome side pipes, and stock Ford hub caps on original equipment tires up front. It sounded really cool, but the lack of consistency in tires and rims and need to shift on the bench seat just did not get the girls excited. I would get the occasional boob graze going into third gear for the girls who sat next to me, but as often as not, was rightfully accused of painfully elbowing my girlfriends in the hooters while shifting. I finally did get the front rims changed over with a matching pair of L-60's by the time I graduated so all my tires matched, but did not get the bump in the hotness factor I had hoped for. The great irony of our ride rejection was that one of the girls who turned us both down drove an AMC Pacer – the car that redefined ugly vehicles for all time. Go figure.

I played halfback on offense. My forte was blocking and receiving. I was not exceptionally fast and very small to be playing the game. At the time I weighed 128 pounds butt naked and wet, but bench pressed 260 pounds. Pound for pound I had the juice and a big heart. I just had no speed or natural talent. The really cool thing about being so small is that 99% of your opponents underestimate you based on simple appearances. That created opportunity and some really fun moments when the big guys could not get low enough to play my game. The other 1% of the time, I just got my ass knocked clean off.

For those of you who do not know how the "center to quarterback" exchange works in football, here's a quick tutorial. The quarterback either gets the ball snapped to him "under center" or "shotgun." We sucked at the shotgun snap because Goob couldn't hit the broad side of a barn, and the shotgun was not in vogue in northeast Arkansas among division 2A schools in 1977. When the quarterback is under center, he places his hands under the center's crotch and presses the top of the upper hand against the top of the center's butt or does the homophobic no-contact with any nuts or ass air pose with his hands just under the center's crotch.

It was early in the third quarter, and Coach had called in a running play where I was to block the right linebacker. The center would snap the ball and stuff the nose guard while the right guard would pull out to block the defensive tackle on the right side. My job was to take down the right linebacker, who would inevitably try to shoot the gap where the guard was. The number two back (otherwise known as the tailback, and the one with speed and natural talent) would get the ball, hit the hole off my right ass cheek, and go where

I and the rest of the defense weren't. It was second down and we had been having a blast that night, ahead by two touchdowns. One of the touchdowns was on a pass play from Roger to me that was epic (I actually caught the ball and made it to the end zone without falling down or making a dramatic dive for the five-yard line). Roger called the play in the huddle, yelled "ready, break," and we hustled out to our positions.

Roger walked up and placed his hands under center and yelled out, "Down," and held a pause to keep the defensive line from catching on to his timing and getting the jump on the offensive linemen. It was almost dead silent in that moment; the tension was palpable as we all tensed up, ready for the count and controlled violence that would follow. "Set" was the next call to freeze and prepare to launch the fury of twenty-two adolescent teenagers who saw the high school gridiron as the canvas for all life to come. At that moment, every player was at the peak of energy at rest. Each gridiron warrior was tensed, taut, and ready to launch. With each exhale of breath, the steam rolled up and over their helmets. No words, no noise, just pure energy at rest, ready to explode. And then it happened.

Amidst the tension there was the sudden, unmistakable sound of air and watery shit competing for a rapid exit from the same orifice. Goob, the center, had sharted above Roger's outstretched hands. For the shit novice, a shart is really a "shit fart" that goes beyond air to spontaneous solids or liquids. Being the consummate professionals we were at the time, nobody said a word and we held our stances. Roger, the coolheaded quarterback, held on for a New York second, then the funk from Goob's ass assaulted his sense of smell. Roger screamed to the top of his lungs, "Damn it, Goob, you shit yourself!" At that instant the entire offense collapsed onto the field in uncontrolled laughter. I forgot to mention that we were wearing white uniforms that night. And right there in the center of Goob's tidy white football pants, square in the ass, was a brown stripe. He had indeed sharted himself. The referees were merely watching the game clock tick down as we all looked like spastic idiots rolling around and laughing uncontrollably. Suddenly, we heard the whistle and heard the ref call delay of game penalty number one.

Coach screamed at Roger to get his ass over to the sideline and explain what was going on. Roger always had a certain look that always showed his anxiety. Eyes open a little too wide, non-blinking, and eyebrows raised high. I could see it on his face as he ran off to the sideline. Roger gets over to the sideline and Coach was livid. When Coach got really good and pissed, he would spit and slobber while he was yelling, with a bit of foam accumulating on the corner of his mouth.

"What the hell is going on?" he yelled at Roger.

"Goob shit himself," said Roger.

"I don't give a shit if he shit himself, get your ass out there, take that snap and play ball!" screamed Coach.

"I'm not touching his ass, he's got shit in his pants," said Roger with a look of pure panic.

"Take the damn snap or you're on the bench!" declared Coach, with a little foam on his lip for effect.

Roger spins and heads back to the huddle. Some of you may know that the center usually calls the offensive huddle. While Roger was over bonding with Coach, Goob did what any good center would do and walked back ten yards and said "huddle up." The stench was eye-watering and kept the huddle looking more like a loose general gathering. Goob said, "Sorry guys, couldn't help it, let's huddle up." Roger runs back into the huddle, catches Goob's odious emanations, and says, "Goob, I'm not touching your ass so snap it really low."

It is at this point that Buffalo Butt comes back into play. This guy found all things crude to be insanely funny and could never let anything go. Buffalo Butt suggested that Goob just line up backwards with his ass pointed at the defense and hand the ball to Roger to keep the defense back. The guys on defense had still not quite figured out that Goob had actually sharted; they only thought he had farted.

Roger called the same play, so we broke the huddle and got into our positions. Roger was holding his breath and placed his hands a couple of inches away from any contact with Goob's newly soiled white football pants with the lovely brown hash mark that seemed to be getting wider with every passing minute. He turned back to look at me in the backfield and take a breath, eyes all googly and focused so he wouldn't pass out from holding his breath while calling cadence. Roger then turns back to face the defense. "Down." Another random pause. "Set." The night was filled only with the sound of the occasional breath taken in anticipation of unleashing hell on the opponent. I could see Roger turn his head to the right and inhale for the final "hut," and he held it just a moment.

Pffssrrrrttttuuuurrrrttttssss burble, burble, pfeeeeeet, poooooooofft, phraaaak, ssssssspht. Goob had let off one of the longest, wet ass, bathtub bubble farts I have ever heard in my life. Roger jumps back into the shotgun position, keeping his cool but clueless as to how to get the ball. Then Buffalo Butt breaks into uncontrolled laughter and collapses on the line of scrimmage. As if they were choreographed by the New York City Rockettes, the rest of the offense collapses down on the turf again into eye-watering, face-hurting, teeth-chattering, gut-aching, sucking-for-air laughter. And this time, the defense had caught on and they too dropped to the turf in the pain of laughter that could not be held back. We were all one in the moment. The only guys left standing were the refs. Everybody else was on the ground laughing their asses off, tears of laughter flowing, and breath coming in spasms. The ref calls delay of game penalty number two.

The ref called an official time out and ran over to Coach, who was at this time drooling, spitting, sputtering, and getting out an occasional sound that resembled words. He had froth on both corners of his mouth. The ref told Coach, "Hey, official time out so your boy can go clean the shit out of his pants. By the way, that'd knock a buzzard off a shit wagon so tell him to clean it good. Five minutes." Coach called Goob over to the sideline and with a foamy mouth said, "Get your ass in there and change your diaper, Goob! (with spittle) And put a cork in your ass while you're at it!"

As Goob headed off to the gym to the lockers, he had to run across the field. At this point everybody in the stands caught on with the telling brown stripe down the ass of his white pants. And the crowd of a couple of hundred die hard Thursday night light fans could be heard roaring with the intensity of Lambeau field on NFL opening day. They also gave Goob a standing ovation. Here on the middle of a damp football field in northeast Arkansas, on a cloudless starry night with a soft wind and a cool forty-five degrees, were twenty-two American teenagers – rivals under any other circumstance – unified by our man Goob and the universal fact that farts are funny and shitting yourself in public is even funnier.

This shit story could have ended here but it doesn't. Goob ran into the locker and was looking for replacement clean white football pants. There were none hanging around in his size. Being the diehard team player, he did what any other committed team player would do. He stuffed his pants with Kotex feminine napkins from the girl's locker room to absorb any further hash mark expansion. And not just a little bit. When he emerged from the gym, the first sign of trouble was the return roar of the crowd and the standing ovation that followed the moment they witnessed what appeared to be an orange and white Jiminy Cricket running out on the field with a one-foot bulge of Kotex extending the contour of the ass of Goob's brown-striped pants. At this point, the coach dropped to his knees and began laughing so hard he was crying. So were all of the referees and everyone in attendance. The game was delayed (by the officials) another twenty minutes while Coach escorted Goob into the locker to clean himself up and he found a dirty brownish pair of practice pants to put on. We won that night but nobody cared. We had just witnessed the greatest moment in northeast Arkansas 2A high school scrub team football history.

As a footnote, I mentioned that Goob was quite a guy. He was diagnosed with Hodgkin's disease shortly after that season and fought through bone marrow transplants and chemotherapy to survive and became a nuclear scientist and Christian missionary. Goob lived to be forty-six years old and died in February 2006. He touched us all as young men and teammates, and went on to live a life of committed service to his God, country, and family. Amidst a shit storm, Goob never lost his cool or his heart. That, my friends, is a true dung beetle.

CHAPTER 3

THE RULES OF DUNG

We've established that shit happens, farts are funny, everybody shits, and sometimes people shit in public. Let's talk about the Rules of Dung.

Rule #1 – Everyone's a shitter sometimes. As much as you might moan and complain about the droppings of others, you leave them around too. At any given time you can be both a shitter and a dung beetle cleaning up someone else's poop. Don't forget this rule because it helps balance you out when you get too involved in the cleanup work you are doing for someone else's droppings. There is a hilarious on-line video of a monkey who climbs up a tree, poops in his hand, takes a sniff, throws his hands back and head up, and falls off the tree. If faced with cleaning up your own poop, the effect would probably be the same. Always look behind yourself and remember, you too have an ass and you use it. In your mind, yours may not stink like someone else's, but it reeks to the rest of us.

Some of you may recall a phrase made famous by General Norman Schwarzkopf during the Gulf War in reference to a reporter's typically wrong assumptions. The general cited the usually exaggerated or incorrect claims of reporters as "bovine scatology." Translated, that's "bullshit." Think back on every time you have been compelled to use that term to describe the droppings of others. And then, remember, you too have left some lying around and been rightfully accused of bovine scatology by those in the know around you.

Rule #2 – If it weren't for dung beetles, the world would be covered in shit. Dung pats would harden, fail to decompose in a timely fashion, and prevent growth. At some point, the volume of poo would exceed nature's ability to decompose it and we'd be in the proverbial "world of shit." Hardened dung pats are great for turd tossing but not much else. I'll have a bit more to say about turd tossing later. Dung beetles keep the cycle of life turning, whether on the farm or in the office. You have to face the reality that you work in it every day and you are either trying to clean it up, standing around the water cooler allowing it to harden, or leaving some around for others to deal with.

Rule #3 – One person's shit is another person's fertilizer. Let's face it, if there were no crap in the government or office to deal with, we would not need all these special skills to work through it and clean things up. Dung beetles need poop and poop needs dung beetles. Watch out for dung beetles who fail to understand that there is always opportunity out there to do something. Shit means an opportunity to apply all those skills you have developed over your life. Wishing there was no crap to deal with will never change the reality that if you're alive, you're leaving droppings around and so is everybody else. Big piles of poop need hard-working dung beetles.

Rule #4 – Dung beetles have to eat to live. Put another way, if you find yourself always on the poop delivery side of the equation, you will not survive. You have to eat a little and do some hands-on rolling to survive. You have been exposed to executives and managers who seem to do nothing proactive or positive, and eventually move on. This is an organizational circle of life reality. If a leader is not eating or rolling some shit balls from time to time, they are not going to be there very long. The shelf life of the perpetual shitter who never dives in to roll one is usually less than thirty-six months (based on my keen eye and federal executive loser history).

Rule #5 – There is always competition for dung. No kidding. It doesn't matter the aromatic intensity, texture, firmness, color, location, or size of the pile – dung beetles will fight over it. I'm sure you have witnessed some suck-up schmoozing an elephant that dropped the mega-turd. A suck-up schmoozer generally does not exist alone and often spawns a geometric progression of suckmeisters who want to get ahead regardless of the nature of the poo. You have no doubt witnessed "groupstink," my variation of "groupthink" wherein a body of otherwise normal professional dung beetles all line up behind the biggest pile of meaningless shit you can imagine and tout its goodness and defend it to the masses.

If you want to see Rule #5 in action, you need only turn on your television any day of the week and listen to the crap being reported on, and the reporters who storm around the fresh stuff. Don't get me wrong, reporters have a very important job and are as essential to the circle of life as the crap itself. The problem is that there is a world of positive, good, extraordinary stuff happening out there every day, but all the rating evangelists want to report on are the negative, scary, and extreme items that appeal to the same masses that cause traffic jams, rubber necking at the latest carnage or some poor schmuck changing a tire on the interstate. Even more annoying is that people pile onto what they see on television or read in the newspapers, accept it as the truth, and form their opinions accordingly. If you have shit on the left, and shit on the right, in the end it's just a shit sandwich with you in the middle. As a general rule, the more passionate a person is while trying to make me see their political point, the more likely I am to ignore them because an unbalanced political shitter cannot be trusted. For all you Democrats, Republicans, Libertarians, and Independents out there, bear witness to this fact – we are all full of shit sometimes, and nobody has a lock on the truth in complex political and economic circles. The sooner we stop acting like one side or the other owns the truth, the sooner we can get to digging into the dung and finding the diamonds that are in there.

Rule #6 – Dung balls attract attention. As soon as a dung beetle emerges from the steamy mass with a nice, symmetric ball, it will get noticed. This rule is important to remember for all of you rollers out there. You are the innovators of the dung beetle workforce. You rollers have the work ethic to keep diving in and getting down to business, while others sit on the sidelines and wait on you to come out of the pile with a nice clean target. The other point to this rule is that if you are working, you and your work will get noticed. Either by the beetles who don't like what you are doing to the productivity bell curve, or managers who want to take your brilliance and their careers to the next level.

Rule #7 – There is a zen to when. Timing is everything in the dung beetle world. Strategically timed droppings are sometimes meant for good, and other times meant for distraction and bad. Random, uncontrolled poorades (my term for a poo tirade) tend to just make more work. It keeps dung beetles busy for a while but in the long run, rule #4 kicks in and the poorader will move on or the company or organization will go out of business. All of you innately understand the power of turd timing. On a simple, remedial level, you can equate driving down the road prairie dogging (when you are teetering on the edge of shitting yourself) and holding that urge until you can find a toilet somewhere or a long-deserted stretch of woods to drop the load. Shitting too soon is, well, sort of like Goob's effect on Thursday night football. Shitting at the right time under the right circumstances is simply a relief.

The more common extreme of this rule is brought to light with the "three-lined potato beetle effect." The three-lined potato beetle larvae carry feces on their backs to prevent predators from eating them. This effect is similar to the tactics I have seen with a number of federal employees. The more trouble they cause with equal-opportunity complaints, unfair labor practice claims, and lawsuits, the more likely they are to be left alone or put off to the side or promoted into a meaningless, no responsibility job. Not surprisingly, this "hands-off" outcome is exactly what they had planned on, and the three-lined potato beetle bureaucrat can live the good life alone in the corner with no accountability.

Rule #8 – Everybody is an asshole sometimes. At some point in every dung beetle's career, you will transition from being the one talking about the asshole to being the asshole. You cannot please everybody, and somebody is always pissed off about something you said, didn't say, or something you did or didn't do. The trick is to be fair, firm, and consistently act for the right reasons and for the long-term good of your dung beetles and organization or company. If you ever follow politics or get involved in politics, rule #8 applies. Almost every decision made by a manager, executive, or politician pisses off a substantial percentage of the masses. Dung Beetle managers must have thick shells and remember to hold steady in the face of the shit storm that often follows any significant decision. And remember Rule #6. If you are really working and making a difference, you will get all manner of positive and negative attention from all sides. It's just the way it is. If you are in a management or executive position and worried about what people think about you as a person, or how they feel about you, you are destined to being bounced around like a turd in a tornado.

Rule #9 – Know your turd types. Dung beetles who do not distinguish between bird shit bombs, rabbit turds, cow manure, and elephant piles are destined to waste valuable hours of their lives taking the wrong approach to poop. All poop is not created equal, and the most effective techniques for dealing with it depend on its nature and timing. Bird shit bombs are made to wear you down. Rabbit turds are an irritating nuisance but usually harmless. Cow manure is benevolent but makes for a lot of process improvement workload. Elephant piles suck up a lot of energy and require more strategy and tactics to resolve. We will go into greater detail later in this book on the turd types and their significance to the Dung Beetle manager.

Rule #10 – Know your dung beetles. If you do not take the time to get to know the people you work with both up and down the organization, you will never achieve greatness. Trust comes from open, honest exchanges from a position of respect and shared vulnerability or hardship. Fear sometimes works in the short run but generally doesn't serve the long-term good of the dung beetle community. I have heard some leaders say "kill one, inspire many" to make the point that if you "fire" (in the military, that usually means a reassignment or retirement) somebody to make an example of people who don't follow the party line, it will motivate the rest to get in line. This is somewhat related to another quote from a marine colonel dung beetle who said that the most successful leaders and teams are "honed in the furnace of hardship." Shortly after he said that, he asked his general for permission to inflict physical harm on a young navy senior executive he was working with who had not yet mastered the zen of dung beetle management. By the way, his general concurred and just asked the colonel not to use any government-issued weapons. The colonel said the permission to cause bodily harm was enough to restrain his desire to actually do it. If you cannot force a behavior change any other way, sometimes you have to unify the masses by sending a few heads rolling to break the inertia. This is not a technique to be used repeatedly or nobody will want to work for or with you. I have never had to go to this extreme in my career, but I have known many who did. As a general rule, it is not a good long-term strategy.

Rule #11 – If you shit on someone's ice cream, they won't eat it after the turd melts off. Put another way, the idea of poo sometimes outlasts its reality. A real dung connoisseur understands both the value and risk of turd tossing. Turd tossing is one of the most critical management tools the Dung Beetle Manager must master. You have to learn when to hold, toss, or shine, and what to throw it on to get the results you need. I heard a story about a chaperone at a high school dance who witnessed some teenagers pouring vodka into the punch bowl. This chaperone cleverly passed his strategy to the other adults at the dance and deposited a fake plastic turd in the punch bowl. Nobody reported the turd because they knew that the spiked punch would also be discovered. As a result of this fake turd toss, nobody else took a drink from the punch bowl that evening, and none of the kids went home drunk from anything the chaperones could control. If you get to the point of throwing a turd on something, someone, or a situation, you just have to remember this rule. The ghost of your turd will outlive its reality. As further evidence of this rule, during the recent bailout bill debate on the House floor, Paul Broun, R-Ga., said of the package "This is a huge cow patty with a piece of marshmallow stuck in the middle and I'm not going to eat that cow patty." The honorable gentleman from Georgia gets it. Turds can be polished and made to look good, but they're still turds.

Rule #12 – God gave us piles of manure so we could learn how to dig. There's a country song that says God gave us mountains so we could learn how to climb. I offer my apologies to that songwriter for this variation on that otherwise aesthetically pleasing way of stating this rule. This rule acknowledges that if we never had to work to roll the big ball, we'd all end up dead. Imagine if all dung beetles did not have to dig, roll, or fight. No poo would be moved and the world would eventually be covered in shit, and we'd all die from all manner of disease or overcome by inertia. Can you image a thousand ants kicked back on a log talking about how great it is not to have to move anything down that damn hole? We'd have less of an ant problem, but a lot more decaying matter lying around the yard. It's the same principle with our dung beetles.

Rule #13 – There are always diamonds in the dung. I read this reference in the preface to the Jefferson Bible while visiting Monticello, and it resonated with me. Jefferson was a student of the Bible and over time, sought to extract out the words of Jesus from the "artificial vestments in which they have been muffled by priests." He went on to say, "There will be found remaining the most sublime and benevolent code of morals which has ever been offered to man. I have performed this operation for my own use, by cutting verse by verse out of the printed book, and arranging the matter which is evidently His, and which is as easily distinguishable as diamonds in a dunghill." Whether you believe in Jesus Christ or not, you cannot argue the power of "love thy neighbor" and His hanging out at the water well with hookers, tax collectors, and other misfits whose unique skills were necessary to change the world. Everyone brings something to the table. The chronic naysayer, the cynic, gripe, bitch, asshole, realist, roller, dweller, or tunneler that you have been in meetings with can be your best ally on the really big dung balls. They drive you to do your homework and set the bar really high for you to convince them that you have something on the table worth pursuing. This is true even when they cannot be convinced of anything of value. At the other extreme of the cynic are the ass-kissing, suckmeister clones that agree with everything and increase the momentum from any shred of support offered from somebody they wish to impress.

My dad once told me there is dignity in all work, no matter how great or small. If the beating of a butterfly's wings in Africa can sow the seeds for a hurricane in the Atlantic Ocean, the guy who cleans the bathrooms at work can set the tone for a really good day that could inspire someone to do something great. Love your dung beetles. They can be a real pain in the ass, but so can you.

CHAPTER 4

BIRD SHIT BOMBERS

This chapter will begin the introduction to the turd types and those who leave them. As you wade through the daily grind, it is important to know what is being left around you and some strategies for working with it or through it to make things better. I have had the privilege of working with a lot of pilots in my career. There is a natural class structure in the naval aviation ranks from the rotor heads, to fixed wing, and the elite-of-the-elite fighter bubbas and bubbettes. Rotor heads "do it in six degrees of freedom," meaning they are nothing but "assholes and elbows" controlling the aircraft in all axes of motion simultaneously. I have heard helicopter and Air Force B-52 pilots use the analogy that flying those aircraft is like a monkey having sex with a football. Fixed-wing pilots are more prototypically balanced, low key, and well mannered, but with many exceptions to all rules. Fighter jocks and jockettes tend to be higher maintenance in all areas with high regard for themselves and their superior aero-intellect and skills. You would not want them any other way, and thank God we have people like these serving our country. The story I am about to tell is compliments of the U.S. Navy fixed wing, P-3 Orion community.

Floyd was a navy commander from the P-3 community. He is of small stature, with some suggesting that he had a Napoleonic complex. Floyd and I worked in a local "think tank" organization that was challenged with doing all manner of the unusual and unexpected for a navy organization. It should be noted that Floyd was the number two man in our little "think tank." Floyd and I were working on a project that required us to visit Wright Patterson Air Force Base. This act alone was a little out of the box for navy guys to go benchmarking against the air force. The afternoon we arrived, we had just enough time to run by the museum there and saw the impressive array of air force aircraft. Floyd kept noting how the air force seemed to pay more attention to creature comfort in all aspects of their business, including putting decent shitters in their aircraft. I inquired why that was of such interest.

Floyd was a tactical officer on the Navy P-3 Orion. The P-3 is a land-based, long-range anti-submarine aircraft. Land-based and long-range means it makes some really, really long flights. According to Floyd, the P-3 Orion had a shitter, but it was known to have problems containing the aromatic fallout from any deposits and occasionally did not flush. So the rule in the P-3 community was that if you were dumb enough to shit in it, you had the dubious task of cleaning it out. And if you stunk up the airplane, you were buying all the beer for the entire crew for the next liberty. In lieu of using the government-provided P-3 shitter, the legend was that diehard Orion warriors used the "shit can," which was really a small coffee or tobacco can with a lid on it for the low-bowel or bladder-tolerant weenies that could not hold it. I have never pissed or shit in a Prince Albert tobacco can and have never met anyone with that level of precision in directional turding, especially while bouncing around in the sky. When I was a kid, I did knock over my grandfather's Prince Albert tobacco can he used as a late night piss bucket, but that's another story for another day.

The P-3 bubbas had a "hash mark" award for anybody who shit their pants while on the aircraft, and the story was that everybody eventually shit themselves or got shitter cleaning duty on a P-3 at one time or another. The only hash mark award I ever saw was in fact a pair of boxer shorts with a real or imaginary brown stain in the back, mounted in a shadow box.

On this trip, Floyd and I were staying at a luxuriously equipped (compared to navy standards) officer's quarters, which happened to be across the street from the golf course. In addition to nice quarters and aircraft amenities like shitters that worked, the air force was reputed to build all the golf courses, barracks, commissaries, and other niceties of life, and only then put the money into the hardware (e.g. airplanes). Floyd felt compelled to educate me on the air force model of amenity building, so we grabbed a six pack of beer from one of the fully stocked refrigerators in our room and took a dusk stroll on the golf course to admire the air force amenities up close. Neither one of us had changed clothes yet, so here was a navy commander in summer whites, and a sand crab (navy civilian) in a suit carrying a six pack walking on the golf course as the sun was going down. Floyd had only drunk two beers at the time of this event so the behavior discussed in this book can only be described as natural for him. In my experience with naval aviators, it would be natural for most of them, including women. We had walked past about four magnificent golf holes and were admiring the housing when we came upon a facility that resembled a club house. It was getting dark and we were down to two beers between us and Floyd needed to piss. Floyd walked up to the back entrance of the club and started pounding on the door. Suddenly, sirens went off, flood lights came on, and we realized the building door had several stars on it – some general's quarters. We hauled ass and dove into a sand trap about fifty yards from the general's house. At this point I had to ask Floyd if it seemed a little weird to be doing this. He agreed that sitting in a sand trap on an air force base, in the dusk, with base police converging on our location, dressed in navy summer whites with a sand crab wearing a suit, was a little out of the norm. So we did what all good navy pukes do and finished our beers while maintaining full stealth in our hiding place. As soon as it was quiet again and fully dark, we slithered out into the evening and strolled back to our barracks. But before we left, Floyd did the honorable thing for any navy pilot in this situation and took a piss in the U.S. Air Force sand trap.

It is an appropriate transition from the naval aviation story to the shitter type known as the bird shit bomber. One need only observe the defensive tactics of the fieldfare bird to get the point. When a fieldfare bird is threatened or attacked, the flock of birds will line up with military precision and begin a well choreographed strafing run of shitting on the offender. Eventually, the offender will tire of the stink and mess and move on. Another variant of the bird shit bomber is the seagull. You may have heard of the seagull management technique that is used by executives or the workforce to fly in looking for a handout, shit all over everything, and leave. If you are walking down the hall and hear someone say, "I've had enough of this shit," you can guarantee that the bird shit bombers have been in action. Watch any political ad two days before any election and you will see nothing but bird shit bombs being lobbed at the opposing candidates. Watch any innovator jump out of the box and throw a radical new idea on the table and see how fast the bird shit bombers swarm and try to choke the passion for change.

Bird shit bombers are strong in numbers, and are everywhere. Bird shit bombers are always shitting on progress or anything that changes the status quo. You will find that most bird shit bombers are usually senior dwellers who like the shit they live in or empire they have built and do not wish to see it changed. Bird shit bombers like to take things out of context, spin the truth, and distort reality. They count on a market of imperfect information to misdirect and keep doubt among the masses.

The dung beetle manager must learn the strategies to avoid the effects of the bird shit bombers. When the dung beetle manager has a great idea or innovative concept to improve the status quo, he must strategically enlist the support of known bird shit bombers. Bird shit bombing tends to build off a mob mentality. One or two shitters lob one in, and if nobody jumps in to stop it, the volley quickly escalates until the original thinker is covered in shit and tires of the assaults. The dung beetle manager must understand this mob mentality and strategically enlist the support of one or two known bird shitters who have the greatest potential to throw up the bullshit flag and stop the assault once it gets underway.

For those readers who have also read the Holy Bible (but will never admit to reading this book), you surely recall the New Testament story of Saul of Tarsus, who was a Christian-persecuting murderer. Saul (aka Paul) was on the road to Damascus and was blinded by Jesus. He experienced a vision of Jesus, became a prolific missionary, and wrote a large portion of the New Testament. With the widely known Christian persecutor standing beside the Apostles, the most likely bird shitters had to take pause and listen. There's a time and place for enlisting your enemies and opponents, getting them on your side, and having them at your side to fight the good fight. Sun Tzu advised keeping your enemy spies close so you could keep an eye on them and in case you needed one to haul a stinker back to the other side for strategic advantage.

I have extensive real life experience in dealing with bird shit bombers. Very early in my career, I had an experience that drove this behavioral model home. I was working as an economist performing a cost-benefit analysis on a navy program and was briefing the customer on my analysis. The analysis clearly showed that there were efficiencies to be gained by making changes to this program. During the brief, everything was going well as I walked through the background, problem, methodology, assumptions, and procedures used to get to the results. I then displayed a slide showing the relative value of various parts of this program and the bird shitters swept off their perches. The first assault was that the data I used was bad. After explaining that the data in question was provided by one of the bomb lobbing shitters, wave one was survived without a direct splat on me.

Wave two came in the form of an assault on my analytical integrity and technical background to be doing such a study. After explaining that I was trained as a statistical economist with a graduate degree, that wave was also put back in the corner. Wave three was launched alleging that I must have manipulated the data. After showing the group the actual file I had received and revealing that the only "edits" had been done by the contractor who provided the data (he had marked records for deletion but in the old Dbase days, you had to "pack" the file to actually delete the records), that wave was squashed.

The last wave came several weeks after the briefing in the form of a Congressional inquiry (strangely, the congressman from the same district as the contractor who had failed to "pack" the records he had attempted to delete). The inquiry alleged that I had used the wrong data and held a pre-established bias against the contractor. Concurrent with that inquiry, the other bird shit bombers came rolling in again and the only thing that put them back in the tree were cold hard facts that could be verified and independently validated.

The object lesson of this experience with bird shit bombers is to make sure you have your shit together when suggesting change in an organization. Ideas without grounding facts are considered to be hallucinations and can be picked apart in a market of imperfect data. Ideas with data but no funding are just visions. Ideas with data and funding are projects to be worked but still require strong advocacy and leadership to see them through. Even if you get to that point, you can expect round after round of bird shit bombers as you approach success. What I find most fascinating is that after all of that shit bombing, the bombers will credit themselves for how well their critical eye and skepticism drove the excellent outcome you undertook. The irony is that there is a measure of truth to that. Remember the rule that there are always diamonds in the dung.

Even if the dung beetle manager cannot find supportive bird shit bombers as allies, there is another strategy to deal with them. An ounce of demonstration is worth a pound of briefings. Even the diehard bird shit bomber will pause and watch a demonstration of brilliance, even if it is two lines of code and mock-up deep. I have found that if you pair up a tunneler with a roller, you tend to get to a product much quicker. I usually find the best tunnelers in the engineering and scientific ranks and best rollers in the program management ranks.

Bird shit bombers are very quick to mob briefings of concepts and generalities because a lot of words and pictures do not have the power of a simple demonstration of a great idea. I have witnessed too many times that a briefing can take on a life of its own and get a lot of attention, but when the chips are down, you have to turn the ideas from the briefing into reality. Really crafty bird shit bombers will keep the unsuspecting dung beetle manager busy doing multiple presentations and revising the briefings, while establishing a mob plan and shitting an insurmountable wall around the innovating dung beetle.

I have a good example of the power of demonstration to share. When the Internet was just taking off back in the early nineties, I was one of the early adopters of this new and unproven technology. We were putting together a Web site to serve as a national clearinghouse of information for defense-training professionals and contractors. My initial budget to prove this concept was a whopping ten thousand dollars. I found a university team who was also experimenting with the World Wide Web and Internet technology, and we put together a wire frame of the site and established two fully populated paths of information through it. The rest of the concept demonstration was pure search engine magic. We put a skin on a simple search service and passed the parameters to a commercial search engine. At that time we were not smart enough to understand the fine art of local caching for demo purposes, so we were going to do this demo live via a dial-up modem. Modems and dial-up Internet protocol technology in the early nineties were as reliable as diarrhea, so this was a calculated risk. The audience for our demo was a couple of navy admirals and a member of the Senior Executive Service. The first demo was a smashing success as we drilled through a rich sequence of information and then passed search parameters to a commercial site and began hopping around the world with more and more facts.

Our next round of demos was in the Pentagon, but we hit a technical snag when we had to run the phone cable almost fifty feet across a hall since the only conference room we could get had no external phone line. In order to get it across the hall without having people tripping on it, we had to tape the phone line up on the walls and run it over the electrical conduit along the ceiling. At demo time in front of a room filled with twenty flag officers, we could not get the connection to establish. The navy captain I was working with tossed one of the shiniest turds I have ever witnessed and claimed that the site was live and the sudden surge in user demand had exceeded our access limits and locked us out. What he didn't say was that the electromagnetic interference from running an unshielded phone cable over electrical conduit, combined with the signal loss from such a long cable run interfered with the carrier signal and that was not a viable technical solution for doing live demos. After that day, we always had our full demo cached to a local hard drive and I carried around a reel of one hundred feet of shielded cable in case we needed it. A sign of preparedness is a guy walking to a demo with his own reel of shielded CAT-5 LAN cable cut to work with RJ-45 phone jacks.

Another time in my career, I found myself on the bleeding edge of progress in low-cost simulation. We had been working on techniques to "shed" workload from high cost training assets (e.g., from airplanes to high fidelity simulators, from high fidelity simulators to low fidelity simulators, and from low fidelity simulators to computer-based gaming and multimedia). My tasking was to explore the low fidelity end of the curve. I conducted a lot of research on the effectiveness of low-cost, computer-based flight simulations and gaming tools and found a formidable body of evidence that those devices actually had positive training value when properly introduced and used.

At that time I was working with a rotor-head (helicopter pilot) navy commander named Mike. Mike was and is a very calm, well-mannered guy. We figured that enlisting a real navy aviator to brief the findings would mollify some of the likely bird shit bombing runs we anticipated. When it came time to brief our initial findings to the naval aviation leadership, Mike was up to the challenge. Our briefing was in the Pentagon, and we witnessed a bad omen before the briefing ever started. We saw naval aviation representatives from the East and West coasts, along with a marine aviator all walking into the room together smiling. For the lay person that would seem to be normal, but in our navy, there are persistent philosophical and doctrinal differences between the two coasts as well as with the Marine Corps aviation community. In those days, they rarely ever agreed on anything. Remaining ever vigilant and fearless, Mike began the briefing and turned from the title slide to slide two, the literature review summary.

A literature review is just that – a review and summary of prior research. Mike began to talk to the bullets (content) on the slide. No sooner than he had opened his mouth on the second bullet, the strafing run of bird shit bombing began from all corners of the room with intensity similar to that seen during "shock and awe." After about thirty minutes of fending off a barrage of personal, professional, and technical insults, Commander Mike gracefully moved off the second bullet and changed slides. The next wave of assaults came in with equal intensity to the first. There was "no way" low-cost flight simulators would be introduced into naval aviation, and any assertion that they had training value was preposterous and faulty. Our team "was out of our swim lane" and "had no authority to be suggesting any changes to naval aviation training." Duh. Our boss was a three-star admiral who commanded the organization responsible for navy undergraduate pilot training. So we ended the brief on slide three of twenty and were unpleasantly dismissed to a cacophony of murmuring about our presumptuousness and the bullshit of the whole idea. The bird shit bombers had put all squadrons in the air and loaded all ordnance. We were fumed away.

The really neat part about being a roller is that if you are rolling for good and for the right reasons, your shell will stiffen and you'll keep pressure on the ball. We did not let that first big wave put us down. We had hard facts that this stuff would work. We kept digging and heard of a young navy ensign who had blown away his classmates in undergraduate flight school by using Microsoft's Flight Simulator to enhance his training. We flew down to Corpus

Christi, Texas, and met with the squadron training officer and this young ensign named Herb. Herb was a history major at the Naval Academy and had no prior flight experience when he joined the navy. Following his selection as a Naval Aviation Officer Candidate, he successfully completed ground school in Pensacola, Florida, then transferred to Corpus Christi to begin undergraduate pilot training. As Herb was progressing through the curriculum, his instructors were all very impressed with his ability to "stay ahead" of the airplane and his knowledge of course rules. In the aircraft, he always seemed to know where the visual cues were. When one of his instructors asked him how many flight hours he had had prior to undergraduate pilot training, he said "none." The instructor did not believe him and said anybody who was that good had to have had prior experience. Herb told the instructor that he had set up flight controls and had modeled the Navy T-34C training aircraft with visual cues into Microsoft Flight Simulator at his apartment. The instructor insisted that he show this arrangement to him, and Herb took him to his apartment. There it was, a simulator setup using nothing other than a home computer, commercial game flight controls, and Microsoft Flight Simulator.

Since we had just been bird shit bombed by our friends in the Pentagon, believed in the power of low-cost simulation, and had found out about Herb's success, we pressed on with a vengeance. With a budget of fifteen thousand dollars, we were at it again. In the strictest engineering sense, we "kluged" together a couple of prototypes using all commercial items and developed the first "micro simulator." We ran a controlled experiment and found that the undergraduate pilots who used our "micro simulator" performed better in the high fidelity simulator and in the aircraft than those who did not. Word got out about this novel approach to pilot training, and our "bullshit" project was featured on MSNBC and in a number of print media. We ultimately managed to get effective low-cost commercial game-based simulators into navy undergraduate pilot training for less than seven thousand dollars per training device. Ensign Herb was awarded the call sign "Hollywood" for his television air time, and because of his superior scores, was offered to fly jets.

Hollywood declined since he almost puked when doing barrel rolls and aerobatics. Herb went on to fly the Navy P-3C Orion and continued on to serve as an instructor pilot back at Corpus Christi. An ounce of demonstration is worth a pound of presentation. Putting a real face on an idea is even better. Don't ever let the bird shit bombers wear you down.

CHAPTER 5

RABBIT SHITTERS

Two brothers from Arkansas are walking in the woods and come upon a pile of rabbit shit pellets. The younger brother asks, "What is that?" The older brother says, "Them's smart pills. You eat 'em and they make you smarter." The younger boy picks up one of the rabbit pellets and takes a bite and says, "This tastes like shit." The older brother says, "See, you're getting smarter already." Footnote for my mother – this short story is not based on personal experience, and I did not talk my younger brother Tony into eating rabbit shit.

The next turd type was a tough call for me. I could have chosen either deer or rabbit shit. I chose the rabbit, but if you're walking in the woods and happen upon a pile of deer shit, you'll get the same effect. Deer and rabbits drop neat little pellets or balls. The feature characteristic of the rabbit shitter is a quick, nervous dump and immediate exit from the stage. Rabbit shitters are the least problematic of all the turd producers. But they are quite prolific and annoying as hell.

When incompetent people are promoted into management or leadership positions, you are guaranteed to find rabbit shit all over the place. The prototypical rabbit shitter cannot find their own ass with a compass and road map, but seem to find a way to needle and meddle in everything otherwise productive employees are doing. These types of employees and managers don't have a clue what they are doing, and are usually too insecure and/or dumb to admit it to anyone. Instead of allowing otherwise talented people the freedom to do what they know how to do, these people run around dropping turds all over everything and everyone, making work where none exists, and keeping everything around them in a constant state of churn. If you have someone in a management position who does nothing but repeat and pass tasking to subordinates without adding a shred of value to the process, you will surely have found a rabbit shitter. Rabbit shitters spend their days keeping the workforce busy, and do their part to keep people in a low level state of non-value-added churn. This gives the rabbit shitter the illusion of power and control since that is the only way they can feel empowered as clueless wonders. One supervisor once showed me a position description that actually said "keep people busy" as one of the duties of the job. The entire position description was written without mention of the critical outcomes and expected product the employees were to deliver. The division head who wrote this position description was the consummate rabbit shitter who spent too many years in the job and eventually won the "breathe the longest" award and was promoted.

The "breath the longest" award is the person who can live inside a steamy traditional Arkansas outhouse in the summertime without going outside or leaving as others enter and do their business. Management eventually appreciates this sense of persistence and loyalty, and offers this diehard, foul air breather an award for their tenacity and loyalty to all manner of stupidity in the face of adversity. They always miss the subtle point that the most brilliant future leaders are smart enough to exit the outhouse before the next customer drops by. Translated for the simple-minded bureaucrat, there are cases where the employee who sticks around long enough will eventually get a promotion. Chronic rabbit shitters are known to file enough equal opportunity complaints or unfair labor practice complaints to annoy management into the age-old strategy of promoting the troublemaker to shut them up and get them out of the bargaining unit. All rabbit shitters aren't morons, but their behavior tends to wipe out any sign of intelligence, and you often end up coming to the same conclusion.

If you have two rabbit shitters up the same chain of command, it can make for many miserable years for the workforce. The best solution for this situation is a change in leadership at the top with a rigid performance-oriented manager who believes in individual accountability and is not afraid to document poor performance. Another approach is for the workforce to push all decisions with any significant accountability up the chain of command so the rabbit shitters themselves will have to be responsible for their actions. The more accountability they have, the less likely they are to continue to meddle in your day job or stick around. Rabbit shitters hate accountability and will go to great measures to avoid it.

In another example, a rabbit shitter was selected to be a supervisor and suddenly wanted every draft, every e-mail, every deliverable, etc., to come via her before it was submitted up the chain of command. The crafty dung beetles around this rabbit shitter called her bluff and flooded her desk with actions and short due dates until she realized she did not have the capacity or interest to manage everyone's job details. This rabbit shitter quickly tired of the pressure from her boss about everything getting bottlenecked at her desk. It should be noted that rabbit shitters are prone to pass blame and toss their subordinates under the bus when the accountability hits the fan. You can only hope the rabbit shitter's supervisor has a clue, but if they don't be sure to keep records, dates, times, and record decisions made by your rabbit shitter boss for reference if you need to counter being blamed for a rabbit shitter boss's incompetence.

Rabbit shitters are also frequently babblers who like to hear themselves hold court. And the content or subject of the babbling doesn't really matter to the rabbit shitter. If you have ever been around a large organization, there is a phenomenon I refer to as the "Biddy Net" (not a gender-specific reference). The Biddy Net is an informal subculture within an organization that is characterized by incessant gossip and bitching about everything and everyone.

Participants in the Biddy Net are usually your most prolific low-level rabbit shitters.

I'm sure you played the game once in your life where someone in a room says a phrase and it gets passed from person to person around the room. When the last person says what they heard, it vaguely resembles the original statement. I was in an executive training course and we were asked to play this game in a smaller group. I did not start the game but understand that the starter phrase was "I like Pooh Bear." The ending phrase in my group was "I have pussy hair." I'm sure some pervert navy commander in the middle of the chain threw that one off. When that game is done around navy guys, marines, or college students, you can expect some severe wordplay. The point is that even a little spin done in progression compounds and masks the original truth.

I have had to revise my definition of "truth" after twenty plus years in the federal workforce. The truth constants in life are the rising and setting of the sun, the laws of physics and gravity, the Ten Commandments, death, and taxes. The rest of truth is an evolving state based on the facts or data known to you at any given point in time. "The Truth" is out there somewhere, but the odds of getting to it economically or in time for it to make a difference decreases as the size of an organization increases. I recall a retired senior executive making the statement that as he moved up in his career, he had experienced a great personal challenge in getting comfortable making decisions with increasingly less time and with less data than the engineer in him would like. He said he never really got comfortable with the model, but learned to stop second-guessing his every move because the truth as he knew it at the point in time the decision had to be made was all the truth he had. The risk was in the cost of delaying a decision versus the additional time and cost it would take to get additional information.

I'm sure I am not alone in averaging almost eight hundred unread electronic mail messages every month. I have access to over twenty different portals, databases, applications, etc., that are "critical" information sources to do my job. And by the way, each has its own login and password, with each expiring in ninety-day windows and with password complexity increasing up to fourteen characters. It is no surprise that the most frequent calls to Department of Defense information technology help desks have to do with password resets or login problems. If you ever saw the introductory video segment for *Get Smart*, imagine if each of the hidden doors had its own login and fourteen-character complex passwords that changed every three months. Old Max would have never made it to the office. It is ironic that with the veritable cornucopia of "information sources" out there, information is increasingly lacking in decision making. The business intelligence segment of industry has emerged to mine the multitude of data sources to provide relevant and timely information for decision makers. The best analysts and decision makers triangulate information from a variety of sources. During war, it is very common that first reports and initial battle damage assessments are misleading. Skilled commanders collect information from a variety of sources to draw conclusions. Human intelligence with boots on the ground is hard to beat. So with all of the technology out there, the most effective sources of information are usually with people "in the know." If you fail to network with people who have access to information that you need to know, you can get tangled up in the technology chasing your tail trying to answer a question that a phone call or visit will resolve.

Dung beetle managers should always strive to get and present the facts and truth to support decisions, but realize that sometimes you are going to get what you get and you still have to make the call. I have seen the risk-avoiding managers get into "analysis paralysis" time and time again and push decisions off long enough so that no decision becomes a decision. Even a non-decision is a decision to do nothing. Zero risk is not an option in the dung beetle world. In my experience, accountability is strongest when the data supporting a decision is wrong or missing. "Drive by" decision making is more common than it should be and is the stuff legends are made of if you get it right. When low data, high pressure decisions turn out to be good, it is expected, applauded, and rewarded. If you get it wrong, the shitters line up, start dumping, and somebody takes the fall. Monday morning quarterbacks have a keen eye for the past, but lack the situational awareness that they were not in the seat at the moment in time under the conditions of reality faced by the poor schmuck who screwed the pooch. That's just the way it is, but the brave dung beetle manager must press on and keep rolling them big balls.

Rabbit shitters are usually just a nuisance, but from time to time executives get sucked into the Biddy Net and professional bias gets introduced into an organization based on nothing but pure fiction and bovine scatology. I have witnessed this over and over where a rumor in the Biddy Net gets a shelf life in the executive library and some dung beetle manager gets plastered with a reputation for things they did not do, or for misrepresentations of things they did. The net behaves like the evening news, looking for juicy morsels related to sex, violence, abuse, tragedy, politics, or other personal drama. Once they get locked on to one, it goes into the net, getting slightly distorted or spun with each pair of flapping gums it passes. Most of the time, this water cooler babble is just that, and has no real effect, but sometimes it influences key people in key places just at a time when the affected dung beetle manager is trying to get something done, and this creates just enough inertia to stop it.

Successful dung beetle managers know that rabbit shitters are a nuisance, and generally learn to just ignore the low-level crap they toss around. If a rabbit turd happens to find a way to stick, you'll find that addressing it head on with facts and leaving it in the dust never to be addressed again is an effective tactic. Watch the best politicians and you will see that they have mastered the art of dealing with rabbit shitters, although sometimes their best approach is to simply ignore the stupid bullshit (e.g., all Democrats are Liberals, all Republicans don't care about the middle class) and stay focused on the things that they believe really matter to voters. The thing to remember is that rabbit shit is really easy to clean up and doesn't usually stick for long.

On a cautionary note, within the federal government, there are so many volumes of rules and red tape that it is rare for people to follow them all to the letter of the rule when doing work. This fact ensures that if you screw up in the government, the potential for making a cautionary tale out of your mistakes is very high. As the ring of visibility to the screw-up expands, the likely outcome will be any number of internal audits, leaks to the media, and from time to time, even our beloved friends in Congress will crawl up your ass with a microscope and find some fresh poo. It is very ironic that Congress pushes for legislation, regulation, and rules measured by the pound, then piles on pork and puts heat on federal personnel to place the funds with a specific contractor in their district. This behavior violates the pounds of rules but gosh darned, nobody seems to care nor can do anything about it because flag officer promotions get held up, funding for weapons systems and national defense gets held hostage, and investigations get started to show the weak what the powerful elephant shitters can do if you dare challenge their inconsistency in public. And if you happen to be the one who gets caught doing exactly what the good congressman wanted, you will get skewered for not following the pounds of statutes, regulations, and policy put in place by our friends on the Hill. I absolutely hate earmarks and congressionally directed funding for those reasons. Freshman congressman and senators show up for work with big dreams to make a difference in people's lives, to assume positions of great power, or for the really cool pin they get to wear. Then they get the object lessons of American politics – pork sells well at home, pork is necessary to buy and sell votes, and on the really big issues of importance to the party, tow the party leadership lines or bills will never find the floor, and there will be really crappy committee assignments coming.

So when you vote to "throw the bums out" and chunk one of your long-standing legislators, you may toss the political baby out with the bath water. The aspiring legislative rookie's voting record will inevitably end up looking like that of the remaining party leadership. So look at who is in control of the House and Senate in the party of your choosing, look at their voting record, and that is what you can expect your newbie legislator's votes to trend toward. That's what makes partisan politics very partisan. To do anything other than vote with the sitting leadership, the newbie legislator becomes cannon fodder, and you'll get squat back home in the old pork barrel.

And the real point to this political segue is that power politics exists in all organizations. Whether it's for votes, committee assignments, promotions, jobs, perks, the corner office with a window, or organizational power and influence, the process is the same. Some get it, some want it, and the rules of the game get written by those who have the power to protect themselves. Wishing it weren't so will never change human nature and American politics.

COW SHITTERS

I actually heard of a proposal to manufacture and install cow ass mufflers to help reduce bovine impact on the environment from cows farting so much methane into the atmosphere. The theory is that all the cow fart methane is eating the hole in the ozone, melting the icecaps, and causing more hurricanes and drought around the world. So for all my friends in New Orleans, the next time you drive by a herd of cows, walk out and slap one upside the head for eroding the ozone and causing hurricane Katrina. But just imagine driving past a farm seeing cows with ass mufflers. That's wrong on so many levels I cannot begin to advocate it. And how would you engineer something that would not cause permanent blockage and injury to the cow? Humans could be next, especially those who like brown beans, onions, and broccoli. On the upside, there are innovative rollers out there working hard to recycle the methane gas from cows into electricity. Cow fart-powered toasters and microwaves are in use today.

Cows are dumb, and there is a magnificent simplicity to the cow. They eat, they shit and are committed to stock a five-star steak house, fast food joints, or your refrigerator. The lucky ones get milked by machines or get to work as studs. If you have ever been driving through the countryside and stopped to watch a herd of cows in action, well, there just isn't much action. They stand around and look dazed. They eat, fart, piss, shit, and sleep standing up. It's all routine stuff, nothing sexy. Cows don't mean anything by it, nothing personal, just ate twenty-five pounds of forage, had some gas, and had to drop the load. They do it so frequently and with such regularity, many organizations hold fundraisers with cow patty bingo where they mark off a numbered grid in a cow pasture, and when a cow takes a dump on the grid, they call it out like a bingo ball popping out. In India, cows are sacred and cow poop is used to make things like detergents, obesity cures, lotions, skin whiteners, and pills for a variety of conditions. In Asia and Africa, houses are also made out of cow dung. So when an Asian or African says a neighbor's house looks like shit, we cannot be sure if that is a compliment or insult.

The point to all of this is that as prolific as the cow shitters are in the workforce, they create what I refer to as the predictable "steady state" stock of routine bovine scat we have to deal with. Typical bureaucratic stuff like the 1940s rule and regulation loving, position description hugging, box checking, buck-passing dwellers who simply cannot find the energy to challenge the terminally stupid stuff dreamed up by other paranoid political machinists who punish the masses for the sins of the few. Government regulation and policies to "get control" of bureaucracies created by the government tend to add layers of bureaucracy, more people with checklists, and generally don't help the end product or taxpayer.

Early in my career there was a process for getting travel approved that required no less than fourteen wet signatures. And if you did not hand carry the travel authorization from building to building, each of those signatures went via internal mail from point to point, often taking two to three weeks for that simple process to complete. We were eventually blessed with some naval aviation roller leadership that came in and asked why we needed all those signatures since only two or three really had any authority to send a person on travel and authorize the use of funds. The process was eventually leaned out to four signatures. We were on a lean, six sigma, total quality leadership roll. But even our esteemed rollers sometimes drop cow turds as a result of a phenomenon I refer to as "leadership overkill." Leadership overkill is simply taking a great idea and overusing and over-generalizing the business case for applying it. It is kind of like the difference between correlation and causation. Correlation is analogous to standing on a street corner, scratching your ass, and having a bird shit on you. You might conclude that the act of scratching your ass caused a bird to shit on you, but you would be wrong. Causation is analogous to standing on that same street corner beneath a flock of birds roosting on the wire above your head and having a bird shit on you while you are scratching your ass. Standing under a flock of birds often causes one to get shit upon. This may seem simple to you, but in the dung beetle manager's world we have an abundance of this level of genius.

Shortly after the great lean event for the travel authorization, our esteemed roller leader (for all you naval aviation pukes out there, he was an F-14 Tomcat driver) had noticed on the facility services invoices that the quantity of toilet paper being stocked was substantially higher on Mondays. This led to a theory that people were actually taking toilet paper home on Fridays or sneaking in on the weekend for some of that low-bidder, high-quality butt reddening paper that you frequently poke your fingers through while wiping the doo, or that tears off one sheet at a time, causing you to just give up and go crusty for the day. This led to my first observed case of "groupstink" when all the senior leadership in the organization went along with the quality study directed by this leader. They collected weeks and weeks of data, poured over the trend lines, and affirmed the good captain's observation that in fact, more paper appeared to be stocked on Mondays. They also found that no paper was stocked on Fridays. It turned out that on Fridays, up to 50% of the workforce was off from the newly implemented alternative work schedule. Since half the workforce was off on Fridays, the stockroom wizard wisely concluded there would be enough toilet paper that day and would do the full restock on Mondays. This way he could reduce the man-hours required for stocking bathrooms and save the government money. Nobody bothered to ask the stockroom manager his opinion, and nobody asked why. If you count up the executive man-hours, the time of the analysts, the time the poor stockroom clerk had to write down all of this detailed shit paper data, we probably could have cut off the business case argument for doing this "study" after the first hour of thinking about it.

Cow manure droppers really don't mean anything malicious by it. They rarely have a deliberate agenda to do harm. They just do what they do and keep the workforce very busy doing non-productive make-work types of activities and make the dwellers feel right at home. Nice and cozy. In any organization that has thousands and thousands of pages of documents providing policy, guidance, and other forms of inspiration, you will find a commensurate quantity of cow manure shitters just blindly following the rules and doing what the standard operating procedure written in the 1940s says you are supposed to do.

Some of you may remember the national shit storm around the $500 hammer. The national media got their hooks into an audit that alleged the government had paid $500 for a hammer. The audit was a flawed interpretation of the contract line item structure and cost allocation by the contractor, but nobody in the media ever bothered to follow up on this fact. The government had taken "delivery" of a hammer, and an auditor asserted that all of the contractor's general and administrative expenses, plus overhead and fees, had to be allocated to the hammer. Regardless of how the imperfect information got out there into the national media, the government's response was to implement a program called "Buy Our Spares Smart," aka the BOSS program. Those in the know called it the "Buy Our Spares Stupid" program. This response to a $500 hammer cost the taxpayer millions for many years and it took almost a decade until somebody challenged the value of having that many people executing checklists before buying anything. Trust me on this, America, the last organization you want investing your money for your future is the U.S. Government. Would you give your money to a charity in which only sixty percent of the funds are actually distributed to those in need? If not, you need to take a real hard look at why you support nationalized health care, entitlement programs, and education spending at the federal level. And just for kicks, take out your pay stub and calculate the total amount you are paying in federal taxes, and then multiply that by your marginal tax rate. That is the amount you are being taxed on taxes paid as if you received that income or those benefits now. There are a lot of cow shitters out there, America, and once you put them in place, it takes decades to get rid of their mess. And they are also contributing to the erosion of the ozone layer and causing hurricanes.

In order to dig out of cow manure, the effective dung beetle manager must wield the shovel of why. Dig up to three layers deep in finding out why things are the way they are. Know who your "Yodas" (the really smart old people who have the corporate knowledge or the process stars) are. Yodas often know why things look the way they do now and provide great context to your line of questioning. Yodas aren't usually the best agents for change, but they are priceless in helping to shape strategies to change the status quo. If you do not challenge the status quo, it will never change without a massive shock to the system. If you are challenging the status quo, dung rules #6 and #8 apply. You will get a lot of attention and you will be called an asshole more often than not. You may even get "fired" to get you out of the way. Get over it and get used to it. America did not get started by a bunch of people who cowered to things that were fundamentally wrong. As you get into higher circles of federal service and even in the private sector, the prevailing personality-driven politics will put enormous pressure on you to conform to a "party line." Anchor your behavior to as much truth as you can, and hold course on what you believe to be right. My rule is to ask how many people have to pay taxes to pay for decisions, and is there a better way to do it? I grew up in a town of three thousand people, plus or minus pets and chickens. That one small town contributed around seven to eight million dollars in federal taxes each year. One decision could effectively commit that single town to pay taxes for decades. If more of our politicians carried around a "tax burden per capita" chart showing how much their decisions added to their constituents' tax burden, they might reconsider some of their votes.

If you have ever walked in a pasture in the summertime, you have also witnessed another interesting phenomenon related to cow manure. If it sits long enough, all the moisture evaporates and the remaining patty can be picked up and tossed like a Frisbee. There are even national tournaments for tossing cow patties. Don't ask why; these same people can be seen at the national lawnmower races or camped out all over cow pastures around Talladega, Alabama, during NASCAR races. I know this because I have had occasion to join the faithful at the annual redneck journey to the holy circle in Talladega. A bit of advice to the faithful: the Old Spice spray that really hot girls hand out will not mask the smell of number two in a recreational vehicle. The real business management point to this is that sometimes, it's all right to just leave some cow manure alone. The quality gurus call it the Pareto principal. Spend most of your time working on higher payoff stuff. Some level of cow manure won't harm anyone, and over time it will just dry up and become another enterprising leader's total quality management or lean, six sigma initiative when the other high-priority scat has been moved off the pasture. In other cases, just as in India and with the energy-savvy farms, manure can be quite useful in productive ways.

CHAPTER 7

ELEPHANT SHITTERS

Early in my civil service career, I worked with a slightly deranged economist (PhD type) who was an army veteran. Rick was a tall, slender guy who had thick Coke-bottle glasses. He frequently pointed out how he needed longer arms to read. This fact is germane to his career progression. Rick was notorious for irritating our boss, a four hundred pound bear of a man named Bill. Rick's antics included tossing and sticking forty to fifty pencils into the yellowing and decaying ceiling tiles in the boss's office located in the old World War II buildings we occupied at the time. The buildings had actually been built by German prisoners of war and had holes in the eves of the roof large enough for birds and squirrels to get in and nest. Some mornings we had to clean the bird shit and rat turds off our computer keyboards and desks. On the odd days when the photo shop next door would process film, we'd get a little buzzed on the chemical haze that would drift into our spaces from next door. Strangely enough, when we had the environmental services folks in to check out the haze, they never showed up during the haze and could not find anything toxic besides bird and rat shit.

One day, Rick was standing in the corner of his office with his back facing the door, slowly pouring a cup of water into one of the five-gallon government-issued green garbage cans (back in the day when we did not have plastic liners) and the water hitting the bottom of the empty can sounded like he was pissing into the can. He sent me over to get big Bill, and when Bill saw Rick "pissing" in the garbage can in the corner he almost had a heart attack. Rick turned around and drank out of the cup for effect.

Rick had a simple philosophy. When working for the government, set your expectations low and you will never be disappointed. He conveyed to me a story about his enlistment experience in the army and why he held that philosophy. When Rick graduated from college, it was near the end of the Vietnam War, and his draft number was such that he was destined for the lowlands in Southeast Asia as a front line infantry grunt if he didn't do something proactive. He had signed up for Officer Candidate School (OCS) and was on his way to becoming an army officer. While at the Military Entrance Process Station, he had been interviewed by a colonel who was a psychologist. This psychologist kept asking Rick if he looked at his shit before flushing the toilet. Rick told the doctor that he did look since it was necessary to ensure that all the stuff you put in actually goes down the hole and does not clog up and cause a flood. This appeared to fascinate this doctor, and he continued to ask Rick details about his time on the toilet. He asked which direction the turds spun, whether they were floaters or sinkers, long logs or small balls, whether he enjoyed the experience, and if he had a good relationship with his dad. Rick was never clear on the point to this line of questioning, but deduced that there must be two types of people in the world – those who look at their shit during flushing, and those who do not. How this actually related to his future assignment in the army was not imminently clear but possibly related.

During his OCS training, he had an opportunity to get out of OCS, convert to an E-5 rank, and go to a job that was less likely to go over the pond and into the soup. He jumped on the opportunity, and when the classifier reviewed his record, which annotated that he had the absolute worst vision possible without Coke-bottle lenses, he was placed into a forward observer job. So Rick concluded that because he watched his shit in the toilet and could not see shit without his glasses, the army felt he needed to be the guy telling them where to shoot. Therein lay the seeds for the cynic I grew to know and respect.

Elephant turds are huge and voluminous. The elephant drops an average of over two hundred pounds of poop per day. Elephant poop is rich in nutrients and can even be recycled into paper. And if you get thirsty enough and find a fresh elephant turd, turn it up, squeeze it, and have an unholy drink on the house. In a real pinch, you can even eat it to survive.

If you have ever watched a parade that includes elephants, you will note a little guy pushing a wheelbarrow and carrying a shovel behind them, cleaning up the droppings. Leaving one of those piles on the road could put a motorcycle down, screw with your mechanic for life (if you ran over it and did not wash the undercarriage of the car), or cause a redneck traffic jam with all manner of roadkill getting run over taking a look at the spectacle.

Surely you get the picture that elephants lay them down large. In the workforce and American politics, there is no shortage of elephant shit to clean up. I'll never forget a navy admiral who told me, "Sometimes I forget when I make a passing statement in a room full of people, somebody takes a note, goes off and starts tasking people to react to my rants and brain farts." As noted by the good admiral, not all elephant shit is intentional. Leaders need to be aware that nonverbal communications, random thoughts, push back on ideas, or even weak or indirect endorsement of an idea often causes the workforce to shift directions when the management team translates it and gets excited. It never ceases to amaze me how otherwise rational and logical humans can sit in a room in the face of overwhelming evidence that a program or initiative is crashing and burning, and still manage to whip out the shinola and start putting a shine on the turd. Believe it or not, a turd can actually be shined. I saw it on *Mythbusters*, episode 113. Jamie and Adam were testing the myth that you cannot polish poop. They applied the same logic and approach as the Japanese dorodango art form, wherein earth and water are molded to create delicate shiny spheres. I also saw an ad on eBay for elephant turd earrings.

Even fossilized dinosaur turds called coprolites are rare and highly marketable. So let there be no doubt that a turd can be shined, both literally and figuratively.

To fully understand how to handle elephant shitters, you must first understand the process of making elephant shit. Elephants eat up to six hundred pounds of food per day. Rabbits – not so much. The digestive cycle time for elephants is relatively short, so they don't have a lot of time to sit around and savor the hundreds of pounds of forage. They have to keep eating and pushing the product through to survive. Elephants see the world differently from the workforce from both a visual and information perspective. Elephants tend to have a "macro," or big picture view, of the work sphere. They connect dots you cannot see, and interpret information with a very different prioritization and filtering mechanism than the average worker or dung beetle manager. Elephants get a lot of data and information that will never be seen by the managers and workforce. It is always fun to play the "if I were king for a day" game. If you dung beetles out there ever get tempted to say, "If I were in his/her shoes I'd......," stop the dumbass game right there. If you were in his or her shoes, you'd have more and different information that you currently have, and would do whatever the information and geopolitical situation at hand warranted. If you had the real facts and did not provide it to leadership, then you would be contributing to the chaos, so it would not be wise to second-guess those who have to act on what they have. Since you're not that king, don't be an idiot and waste the neurons on it. Be the king where you stand and lead from there. Someday, your kingdom will get larger and you'll be the one everybody thinks they would like to be for a day.

The one thing I absolutely admire about the United States Marine Corps is that they generally pick some really good leaders, and when U.S.M.C. leadership speaks, everyone gets in line. If a marine general says a pile of shit is a shiny chocolate substitute, his or her subordinates say "chocolate hooah" and start munching. The downside to this extraordinary discipline and respect for the chain of command is that if the general was wrong, a whole lot of marines suffer and the few and proud who argue the point find their careers end abruptly.

Elephants use all of their senses to navigate, depending as much on their senses of smell and hearing as they do their vision. Our leadership elephants tend to develop multi-sensory capabilities since they process so much data in such short intervals that their instincts often kick in to guide their decision making. Leadership is an earned and evolving quality that one of my marine friends described as being "honed in the furnace of shared hardship." Let's break that down. Honing is a metal-to-metal contact sport. You cannot hide behind e-mail and text messages when the leadership chips are down. Metal-to-metal means face-to-face. If you cannot own your decisions and be accountable both up and down the chain of command, the metal-to-metal contact is brief and dulling instead of sharpening. "In the furnace" means it is hot, and that is where the density, strength, and longevity of the metal is forged. Leaders are under a lot of scrutiny and pressure from internal and external sources. Leaders withstand the heat, hold course, and reinforce the troops to get the job done in the face of overwhelming odds. Remember Rule #8, that every decision pisses someone off. The more people you are accountable for, the more pissing and moaning there is to include demagoguery, lawsuits, and complaints of all types. "Shared hardship" means you've been there, done that, and learned from it. Imagine how effective a football team would be if the first time they put the pads on and got at it was in the first game. How would they know what to do? How would they get to know each other's strengths and weakness? How would they know they could pull together as a team from adversity and meet the challenge? Elephants often are asked to take their shared hardship experiences forward to different people and do not get to keep the same trusted agents with them after going through hardship as a team. You will see a tendency for elephants to bring some of their trusted agents along with them, but it is usually limited to just a few people. The best leaders can apply their skills to new and diverse teams and still make magic happen.

Elephant turds are really hard to toss because they are very large and heavy. Bird shitters leave a mess, but there's nothing to hold onto when they are done. Rabbit shitters drop all these nice round balls and frankly, you could step in them and not even notice. Cow shitters leave a lot of standard stuff around that keeps a steady strain on those doing the work, but they can be overcome with a little extra focus and a rapid improvement event here and there. When elephants drop the load, the fixes and course changes are not so easy to make. In the Department of Defense, there is a flow down from the Administration, to the DoD, to the Services, to the various organizations within the Services, and all the way down to field activities and operating forces. The budget process is based on a six-year rolling cycle in which you have to project spending two years ahead, can make minor adjustments one year ahead, and essentially do the best you can in the execution year. DoD funding comes in "colors" that each have unique rules for spending. My favorite form of elephant weirdness combined with a perma-crust layer of cow shit is when the Defense budget is held up in continuing resolution. Spending is capped at prior year levels and fractionally disbursed. I have seen funding get held up until January (the fiscal year starts in October). So the dung beetle managers are prohibited from spending money on new programs until January, then get slammed during mid-year reviews in March and potentially have their funding pulled back in the summer, since it took too long to spend when they only had the full funding for three months. Meanwhile, the Federal Reserve and Treasury Department concurrently slams the financial markets with seven- or fourteen-day cash management bills and dries up liquidity in the banking system while continuing resolutions are ongoing. During the fall of 1985, I was working as a money market trader and personally witnessed how fast and furious the credit markets tighten up when the government is using cash management bills to finance operations. One day I was in an over-sold position of about twenty million when the alarms went off on our machines and the markets went "suspect." That meant trading was temporarily suspended upon notification that the Federal Reserve and Treasury had just dropped unprecedented billions in cash management bills into the system and basically, everybody went ape shit, so they suspended trading until we could sort out where to restart the bidding. I ended up having to go to the Fed, as the "lender of last resort" to get the cash to balance our overnight position. To go to the Fed, you need your bank president with you, and he's usually not happy about being called in at 1800 hours to argue why he was in such a risky position that he needed Fed help.

For those of us involved in federal acquisition, there is an abundance of elephant doo to deal with. Federal contracting goes in cycles from fixed price contracts to cost contracts and back and forth. To put it very simply, if you know what you want very clearly, and there are precedents in the market for getting it, fixed price contracting is the way to go. Under fixed price contracts, the government assumes very little risk. Contractors, on the other hand, assume a lot of risk under fixed price contracts. If you aren't really sure what you want, and there are few or no precedents for it in the market place, cost type contracting is the way to go. Under a cost contract, the government assumes most of the risk while contractors assume very little risk. Congress advocates broadest use of competitive contracting to get the best prices, but allows sole source and limited competitions to small and disadvantaged businesses. Competitive contracting is best when the product is fairly common in the marketplace but usually takes a minimum of six months from start to contract award, and that is on highly streamlined procurements. The decision on contract type is best left with the acquisition manager faced with the action to go obtain a product or service. It is not a good idea for Congress to legislate contracting strategies and types since the federal workforce is so full of rabbit and cow shitters who cling to their checklists and twenty-plus year old standard operating procedures that are not adaptable to all scenarios. Congress has swung that pendulum back and forth so many times it makes me dizzy. Instead of holding individual acquisition executives accountable when making chronically stupid contract determination decisions, legislators feel the need to spray the entire workforce with poo-be-gone.

In the elephant sphere, and especially in the federal government, once a load is dropped, a lot of effort goes into circling around it and spinning it to be food for the masses, goodness for growth, and a long-standing source of life, including initiatives like branding, total quality, lean, six sigma, business process reengineering, competency aligned organization, balanced scorecard, and any number of other sexy titles. Once a program or bureaucracy gets put into place, it takes at least three years to shut it down – and that is the exception, not the norm.

Once the large load has been dropped, the dung beetle manager has to take a much more strategic approach to cleaning up after elephants. Elephant dung tends to come with political initiative, strings and conditions, high level commitments, strategic communications, and a host of other attributes that make it very dangerous or futile to just jump into the pile without doing your homework. As the implementation sphere expands, the number of geopolitical factors that come into play expands proportionally. For example, making a simple process change within a small organizational unit is a fairly simple process with the coordination and impact of the changes somewhat limited. As the number of impacted elephants increases, the time required to socialize, educate, coordinate, and achieve concurrence on an initiative or idea increases exponentially. I have found that the typical cycle time from the inception of a great idea or plan to the point where it breaks through perma-crust to common understanding and acceptance is at least eighteen months. And that occurs only after holding course through all of the bird shit bombing raids, rabbit turd distractions, wading through cow shit, and the crafty dodging of the onslaught of elephant turds that never ends. If you want to successfully navigate through elephant shit, you'd better learn how to be patient and persistent. One of my favorite high school math teachers had a term called "sticktuitiveness" she used to describe the tenacity and persistence needed to be successful in her algebra and calculus classes. Pilots throughout time have had to hold course through antiaircraft fire with shells and missiles exploding in order to achieve their mission. The dung beetle manager must build the confidence, and have the courage to do the same when trying to clean up elephant turds.

When elephants dance, there is a lot of mass in motion and potential for things to get knocked around. Elephants tend to have a lot going on, and when data gets passed to them that requires their engagement, it needs to be concise and factual. Once the elephants take the data on and start to do something about it, the original facts can get dwarfed in a lack of context, distorted message, or any number of misrepresentations of the real deal. The principle motivators of the elephant are fear, pain, thirst, and hunger. Elephants are trained with an ankus, or hook. Look around your elephants and you will find a "handler" staff. These handlers understand what motivates each elephant, and also possess the hook needed to get the elephant's attention and get them to turn in the direction you want them to go. Before you invite an elephant to the dance, make sure his or her handlers have already been briefed and prepped old Simba for the samba, waltz, or macarena you intended. Otherwise, there will be numerous staffs doing countless cleanup work trying to unscrew the misfire.

Mere facts and compelling data are often insufficient to change course on an elephant dropping. Some of you may have heard of the Base Realignment and Closure (BRAC) legislation passed by Congress back in the early nineties. The intent of this legislation was to study the long-term cost and benefit of consolidating military bases and required an up or down vote on the final package without letting the porkers in Congress meddle with the results and prevent anything good from happening. The legislation was necessary because no congressman worth his or her salt would allow a federal institution to close in their district without a major fight. I was working with a major command in the navy during the 1993 BRAC round and had gone to the trouble of going to Washington and getting the actual analytical model used in the analysis of base realignment and closure options. Some colleagues and I worked up all of the proposed options for closing navy training centers concurrently as the data was being passed to the Department of Defense team that was performing the analysis to present the options. There were three navy training centers in use at that time; one was in beautiful San Diego, California. Another was located in Orlando, Florida, and the other was in Great Lakes, Illinois, just north of Chicago. The navy had a boot camp at each site. Here are a few factoids for each site. The United States Weather Bureau describes San Diego's weather as the closest thing to perfect in America, and there is a large navy presence in the area. Orlando, Florida has a year-round average temperature of seventy-two degrees and is one of the world's most desirable vacation destinations. Great Lakes Naval Station is located on the edge of Lake Michigan, is the farthest away from any sign of the operating navy fleet, and has an average temperature of forty-nine degrees. Now absent any other information about these three locations, if you were a potential recruit for the navy, where would you want to go to boot camp?

As we poured over the data that was being submitted to the BRAC team, we were also loading it into the BRAC cost model. Upon completion of our analysis, we had found that it cost as much to operate and maintain the Great Lakes facility as it cost for both San Diego and Orlando combined. Our data clearly showed that it was less expensive for the taxpayer to close down the Great Lakes training center and move those capabilities to San Diego and Orlando. We briefed our results to the admiral responsible for these facilities and he concurred with our results. The navy submission to the 1993 BRAC closure study from the lowest levels up the chain of command included the recommendation to close the Great Lakes facility and move it to Orlando and San Diego.

In order to fully grasp the elephant sphere on this decision, you have to get a quick geography and history lesson. The Great Lakes Naval Station is just a few miles from the state line of Wisconsin. Les Aspin represented Wisconsin's First Congressional District in the House of Representatives since 1971, and served as Secretary of Defense from January 1993 to February 1994. In March 1993, he was the one responsible for releasing the BRAC plan to close or consolidate major installations and minor facilities. The Great Lakes Naval Station is in Illinois, just north of Chicago. In 1993, Congressman Dan Rostenkowski was the United States Representative from Illinois, and had been on duty since 1959. In Washington, he rose to the rank of chairman of the powerful House Ways and Means Committee in 1981. As chairman of Ways and Means, he played an important role in tax and trade policy for more than a decade.

In 1993, Democratic President Bill Clinton was in office. Both Aspin and Rostenkowski were Democrats. Congressman Duncan Hunter, 52nd District (San Diego), was a Republican. Bill McCollum, 5th and 8th District (Orlando), also a Republican.

On the day the 1993 BRAC list was released, we were stunned. The BRAC committee recommended closing Orlando and San Diego training centers and moving those to Great Lakes. So the Department of Defense (Les Aspin, of Milwaukee, WI, Secretary of Defense) came to the conclusion that our math had to be wrong, and that navy recruiting would be better served avoiding all the distractions of sunny San Diego and Orlando and opted for the frigid climate of northern Illinois to inspire future generations of sailors. I know that Congressman McCollum was originally allowed a brief time slot to present his facts, but was prohibited from presenting any contradicting data to the BRAC committee as the result of some last minute rule changes. I'm not sure if the same thing happened to Congressman Hunter but suspect that was the case as well.

Having served in the navy at all three of those locations, I can say with greatest confidence that Great Lakes, IL, would be one of the absolute last places on earth I would elect to go if I had a choice. When I joined the navy, it was on the written condition that I not go to boot camp in Great Lakes. I ended up in San Diego, and I had mistakenly blazed through my follow-on training and arrived in Great Lakes five weeks ahead of my friends. My smart navy friends spent another five weeks in the southern California sun, and I spent that time freezing my ass off cleaning shitters by hand and serving mid watch (0000-0400) twice a week by walking around frozen buildings in the snow with ice accumulating in my beard. But I did get a really cool honor graduate certificate.

Before diving into an elephant turd, try to put some light in the forest. A blind elephant turd dive is analogous to running through the woods at night without any light. It might sound like a really good idea at first until your face finds a low-hanging limb or the ground disappears beneath your feet and you feel the temporary exhilaration of flight. Your ability to understand the geopolitical parameters around your elephant turd is directly proportional to how much light you shed on it. Dig into the history of the dropping, who wanted it, who didn't, and who has a stake in its future. Find out how high the political support is for it. If you don't have good human intelligence in the right places to provide credible information, you are usually left with public records, and those are often spun or redacted to the point where they are not very useful. Failure to judge the geopolitical landscape will result in failure to clean up the mess.

When cleaning up elephant turds, pace yourself and build a coalition of the willing. First of all, elephant turds are huge and you will burn out trying to move them all by yourself. You will need high-level support to sustain the roll, and if you cannot find executive-level support for your approach, the odds of success fall. If you cannot find an executive champion for reinforcement and guidance, the only hope you have is independently verifiable data and facts, and in extreme cases, the media. I do not advise pulling the media into your cleanup effort if you can avoid it because once that door opens, you cannot control where the story goes or who is impacted by it. If the cleanup effort warrants media attention, you are most likely going to be on your own and subject to all manner of personal and professional manipulation if you remain on the job. The government touts whistle blower protection but in my experience, whistle blowers tend to be treated badly once the genie gets out of the bottle. I really enjoy working with retirement eligible people who get really honest and hardheaded in their old age. They can say and do things the newbie cannot do because they have lost the fear of being fired, since they are working for thirty to forty cents on the dollar anyway.

Retirement eligible personnel with political connections are really good people to know and work with.

Sometimes, the power structure is beyond your ability to influence it, and you have to make a decision about how hard to fight and when to fight another day on another issue. I admire people who hold on principle and values even when the odds of succeeding are minimal. Whether to press into the pile or pass for another one is a personal choice, and there are no firm and fast rules to follow. Whatever course you choose, just be sure of what your motivation is and that you can live with the possible negative ramifications to you personally and professionally.

CHAPTER 8

THE ROLLERS

My friend Jim, aka JB, is an American Hero. JB recently retired from civil service as a member of the Senior Executive Service. I worked with Jim for about twelve years and grew to respect him in every way. JB is an Italian with a huge heart for his country. He was an army medic during Vietnam and saved the lives of many a wounded soldier. Risking his own life time after time to save another, he eventually was wounded and received the Purple Heart. During his time in combat, Jim never received any substantial accolades for his bravery. His commanders felt he needed a break from the front line action and placed him in a position in the rear of the fighting and gave him one simple job. He went from saving lives to being the latrine officer for the unit.

His job was simple: follow the army field manual procedure for pouring diesel into the 55-gallon drums after removing them a safe distance from the outhouse and burn off the shit. Replace the drums and ensure proper stocks of toilet paper and reading material. After doing this menial task for a few months, Jim was called into the commander's tent. He was expecting to get an ass chewing but instead was awarded a medal for his superior service as the latrine officer. Jim graciously accepted the medal and walked into the hot, damp evening full of stars in Southeast Asia and wondered quietly to himself why this particular brand of service caught the eye of his superiors while dodging bullets in combat and saving his brothers barely registered. His conclusion was elegant and simple. Elephants like a clean ass, and expect to have their shit cleaned up. This experience molded his humble and gracious leadership style, and contributed to this man doing more elephant-turd cleaning in the U.S. Navy than anyone I have ever met.

Rollers are among the people you find one or two standard deviations to the right of the mean. They possess unusually effective communication skills and are fearless, aggressive, assertive, visionary, and cannot stand the status quo for very long. They are usually the most effective agents for change and have an uncanny ability to stay on task well beyond the point where most people give up. Rollers are never intimidated by the size of the pile in front of them and have no patience for sitting around talking about how big it is. To put it in terms of one of my favorite roller senior executives, "Forty percent of something is better than one hundred percent of nothing. Shut up and get at it." Rollers somehow instinctively know that as soon as they start rolling the ball, the sideline-loving shit eaters, opportunists, and bird shit bombers are going to pile on and either try to steal the ball or tear it to shreds. And that reality really doesn't bother them. The roller takes it as a personal challenge to be mastered.

I refer to most rollers as "having the disease." The disease is that they are overachievers who stay on task sometimes to the detriment of every other aspect of their life, and regardless of how many obstacles they face, they never give up. Rollers with the disease are "over the horizon" projectiles that a leader need only point in the direction of the objective and stand by to assist in prosecuting the target. Older rollers tend to be very effective communicators, although younger, less seasoned rollers often come across as pompous, arrogant, and abrasive.

Rollers also tend to be highly diverse in their talent. I have seen rollers take on challenges in areas they had little to no experience in and thrive. Like some of the dung beetle population, some rollers are so intent on getting into the game, they ride on the tails of the shitters to minimize the wait time to get to work. They do research, talk to people, and absorb new information like sponges. Rollers connect dots where others cannot and blaze original trails to solutions that drive the checklist huggers absolutely nuts. Rollers seek a quick path to mastery, and if they do not feel competent or up to the task, they are quick to ask for help. Rollers are highly impatient, don't sit idle for long, and usually don't want to stay on any single task, program, or initiative for more than three years. Within the bureaucracy, rollers can move around organizations easily and continue to contribute and raise the bar everywhere they go.

You can quickly identify a roller in a group since they are usually the ones who avoid opening the ten-pound policy and guidance documents and convulse at the idea of having to follow checklists to do their work. Go to any major leadership conference and you'll see common themes that people who go outside the norm are the ones who change the world. America did not happen with a bunch of compliance checkers. Art is not born in a template. Scientific breakthroughs are not achieved by the risk averse. Movement is not possible without motion. The magic is in separating the shit from the shinola. Checklists, policies, and procedures are developed with good intent, and have value – up to a point. They have to be rationalized to the circumstances and time. The spirit of policy and guidance can be kept without getting into rigid, unyielding rules and checklists.

I've discussed the many positive attributes of the roller, but there are less desirable characteristics that come with such intensity and impatience. Young rollers can be quite obnoxious. They lack geopolitical awareness and can be confrontational in the way they challenge the people they work with. With proper mentoring and guidance, they can be unleashed as pioneering leaders. If the dung beetle manager does not recognize the young roller and tries to squash that energy, the young roller will not stick around. If a young roller is prematurely placed in a leadership position, they will usually piss off the entire workforce and fail to remain effective. The bridge between these two extremes is a seasoned dung beetle manager who recognizes the rollers and gets them into a mentoring or development program where their rough edges can be softened. In my experience, the federal government absolutely sucks at identifying and developing roller leaders. The preponderance of cow and rabbit shitters who advance to elephant status like to clone themselves and often see a young roller as a threat on many fronts and deliberately try to put them in their place. The best advice I can ever give the American economy is to identify and develop your young rollers.

Another downside to the roller is the inability to maintain whole life balance. I have seen this over and over and through my own personal experience as a roller. There is some part of our DNA that demands a high personal standard that is continuously raised and never quite achieved. The standard itself can get off course so badly that you begin to believe your own bullshit and that is dangerous. Rollers need friends and mentors around who can raise the bullshit flag and provide course steerage. Rollers need a continuous gut check on their motives to assess if their intensity best serves the customer or themselves, their family or their job, their spirituality or their ego.

As a general rule, you do not want two rollers together in the top two positions of any organization. With two rollers at the top, the challenges to the status quo and lack of stability will cause undue stress and damage to an organization. All change has its own timing. Economists will argue that it is good for Americans to face high gas prices long enough to alter their consumption behavior. This permanent behavior change will, in the long run, reduce future demand and prices for gas. On the other hand, a temporary shock that is perceived to be short-lived will not generally alter behavior. A temporary two-week spike in gas prices is an irritation but if consumers believe it is temporary, they won't change their driving patterns, and will not be interested in a small hybrid vehicle. If, on the other hand, gas prices stay high for several months, that inspires people to park the guzzler and get in the hybrid. In bureau-speak, the dwellers can "outlive" the roller problem if they believe it is temporary. Since most of the senior leadership in the government and military rotates on predictable cycles, the core dwellers just wait it out and brace for the next round of rollers to come in and form up the next ball. That is why it is essential to pair up a roller with a dweller or tunneler at the top of the food chain. Dwellers and tunnelers carry their own unique and extraordinary value to an organization and should never be dismissed by wild-eyed rollers. I'll talk about dwellers and tunnelers in following chapters, but the key message is that they provide a counterbalance to the pace and timing of change. If a dweller or tunneler signs on to the roller change plan, it takes on the appearance of being permanent as opposed to temporary, and people will eventually get that message and get behind the plan and start pushing the ball.

Never ever, under any circumstances, try to micro-manage a roller. Somebody will get hurt or people will leave and you never know who that will be. Rollers need a general target, limited guidance, and an occasional engagement with leadership for steerage and course correction. If leadership starts inducing paper cuts from rules, policy, and guidance without regard to situational relevance, the roller will bleed out or go into a defensive crouch and fight back. When rollers fight back, they are usually very competent in their ability to produce facts and argue their points, so to the would-be micro-manager of the roller, be warned. Don't go there. They can make you look stupid and get you moved into the corner basement office with no windows.

CHAPTER 9

THE TUNNELERS

This introductory story takes me back to my youth. I had a buddy named Joe who was a doctor's kid and lacked nothing in life except for common sense after the marijuana took over his higher brain function in his sophomore year of high school. Joe is the only guy I know who managed to shoot holes in his boat and truck in the same school year and then ended up with a classic 1977 Pontiac Trans Am and managed to destroy that vehicle's transmission in less than six months. The boy had issues with moving vehicles and weapons.

During our freshman year in high school, Joe and I had struck up a good working relationship with the school librarian. During our study hall hour, she would allow Joe and me to sneak into the back office in the library and play chess. I got the upper hand on old Joe when I learned the quick three move technique and smoked him for a couple of days. He decided to retaliate one day and did so by letting off a real sinus-scorching fart. Not to be undone, I fought back with an eye-watering release of my own. This back and forth fart fight continued for about ten minutes. Just as we tired of the battle, the librarian came in and made a contorted face while looking up at the ceiling. She noticed one of the fluorescent lights was out and said, "Boys, I believe one of the ballasts burned out up there. That smell is just awful."

Joe and I were having a very hard time keeping a straight face and continued to play chess as she walked around looking at the ceiling from several angles. She proceeded to call the school custodian who came in within a few minutes, took a quick whiff of the scorched earth odor, and agreed that it must be burned out ballast. The custodian commented, "I ain't never smelled one quite like this, it must have melted some plastic or paint." That one put us over the top and we both almost lost it at the same moment as we stood up with our hands over our faces. The librarian said, "Boys, ya'll need to go see the school nurse and see if those noxious fumes might have affected you." Our eyes were watering from highly restrained laughter and the custodian said, "Boys, my eyes are watering too so ya'll better get on out of here." We left, and the custodian found out that only the bulbs needed replacing. The mystery of the burning ballasts left the school library with Joe and I on that day.

As I've indicated before, tunnelers tend to come from the engineering, technical, and scientific ranks. The uniform characteristic of the tunneler is that they understand the laws of physics with an innate understanding of what is doable and what isn't under any given set of conditions. Put another way, they get shit done. Tunnelers observe the apparent chaos the rollers unleash when they dive into the pile and start rolling. Tunnelers take note of the amount of energy it takes to execute a frontal assault on the pile, and the corresponding energy it takes to successfully emerge and roll through the sideline-loving shit eaters who simply wait on someone else to do the dirty work.

By contrast, a roller is quick to commit to prosecuting a target with all manner of risks and obstacles in the way, while the tunneler will meticulously identify all the steps, risks, work-arounds, and resources, and put together a very detailed work plan. Most of the time, elephants don't like what tunnelers have to say about the way ahead. It takes too long, costs too much, and the approach is too risk averse. Elephants will love the roller answer of "no problem, when do you want it?" but the laws of physics and reality usually do not support such optimism.

Tunnelers will start the seemingly impossible task of beginning to dig straight down under the dung pile with the sideline-loving shit eaters making fun of them for doing all that extra work. The tunneler plods along at a snail's pace, moving small quantities of dirt at a time, continuously making incremental progress downward from the dung pile and down into tunnels underneath. The tunneler's dung ball is not visible to others, so there's not much conflict in the tunnel. In the dung beetle world, the digging of tunnelers and rollers increases aeration of the soil and increases the moisture content, contributing to long-term fertility for future use.

Tunnelers don't get much attention and they like it that way. Tunnelers prefer to work in the background and tend to be very quiet, and left to their own, they are very secretive about what they are doing. Tunnelers "fly below the radar," working directly under the dung pile, and try to make steady progress without undue attention from elephants and others. The advantage of the tunneler approach is that the work gets done well without a lot of distractions and elephant dancing trying to influence the product or outcome. The voice of the tunneler says, "Just tell me what you want done, give me the resources, and get out of my way." All program managers learn that cost, schedule, and performance are continually traded off to make a product or achieve an outcome. The part they do not teach program managers is that politics, economics, and physics are the other three-legged stool you have to balance. Tunnelers perform well when they have a hand in defining the cost, schedule, and performance goals for an effort. When a roller throws in politics and economic artistry, the sanctity of the otherwise well-defined project becomes disturbed and tunnelers become very uncomfortable.

If the world were run by tunnelers, things would slowly and steadily improve. Did I mention slowly? If you ever watched *Star Trek*, Scotty, the chief engineer, was the consummate tunneler, and Captain Kirk was the prototypical roller. The captain would call for warp speed and Scotty would try to explain how long it would take, how risky it would be, and then get told to move the ship or risk the death of all aboard. And the ship would move at warp plus, every time.

Everyone should be so lucky as to have a Scotty on their staff. He'll be the first to throw the bullshit flag at the elephant PowerPoint Rangers trying to make engineering decisions that will consume millions of dollars with less analytical rigor than a drunk uses to decide where to take a piss in the grass. Force of personality means little to the tunneler; he or she is an equal opportunity bullshit flagger and is not usually intimidated by the level of the manager trying to tell them how and what flavor of shit to eat. If you want to see some real entertainment, direct a tunneler to do something on an unrealistic schedule with inadequate resources. In the end, the tunneler might concede like Scotty and go perform a miracle, but not without exposing the very soft underbelly of the unsuspecting leader who tossed the turd their way. It never ceases to amaze and impress me at how much tunnelers get done under ridiculous circumstances without inflicting bodily harm on someone.

The best leadership teams I have observed in my career are usually a combination of tunneler and roller at the top. It doesn't really matter which one is at the top of the food chain as long as there is one of each to counterbalance themselves. I have tremendous respect for the tunnelers who look me square in the eye and tell me my plans are shit, then proceed to fill in the holes with sound logic and physics. People who tell you your plans are shit and offer no value-added input are usually dwellers who spend their lives in the dung pile doing everything they can to avoid change. The enterprising dung beetle manager must be prepared to hear the truth whether it agrees with the direction of the political winds of the time and act on it. The injection of the art of the possible into decision making is the tunneler's forte. Failure to listen to them is a mistake. Doing things their way all the time is a mistake. Somewhere in between the "desirement" and the "requirement" is a solution and a schedule that will be good enough.

The tunneler is often enamored with quality to a point where better can become the enemy of good enough. I have seen this tension throughout my career, and it is constructive up to the point where the marginal benefits of making the next incremental improvement are overcome by the marginal cost to do so. Tunnelers often have no appreciation for the very large gray zone that exists between black and white and have to be led kicking and screaming into the land of uncertainty that comes with everyday leadership. The Department of Defense stresses "operational risk management" as a method to better understand the decision trade space. It is a good model for bridging the communication gap between apparent tunneler absolutes, but is only as good as the rigor placed on getting all the facts. Rollers will tend to take more risk; tunnelers will tend to take less risk. That is why they must be teamed together and led by a dung beetle manager who understands their strengths and weaknesses.

Another less desirable attribute of the tunneler is "analysis paralysis." Analysis paralysis occurs when decisions continue to be deferred as more and more data is collected and debated. This behavior is most prevalent when you have a tunneler decision maker with tunnelers providing the options. Their desire to get it right and preference for quality can drive decisions out to a point where the lack of a decision becomes a decision by default. The solution to this problem lies in mixing up the team to ensure that you have a balance of dwellers, rollers, and tunnelers to allow the creative tension necessary to make a better decision.

There are numerous examples of taxpayer casualties that have occurred when roller leadership has not paid attention to their tunneler teammates. I have personally witnessed about $1 billion of taxpayer funds that have been poured down a dry hole as a result of elephant roller leadership that became enamored with PowerPoint level engineering or their own profound technical knowledge (that typically comes from talking to industry elephants trying to sell their stuff to the government). I was first introduced to one of these programs (that has accounted for over $800 million of "almost finished ware") in 1996. I was at a meeting in the Pentagon in which I was told that this particular program was going to replace half of the systems I was working with, and that no money would be authorized for anything other than this big-bang solution. In

2009, this grand big-bang solution has yet to deliver, while critical modernization efforts have been held up for thirteen years while the never-ending stream of promises have never materialized. In these scenarios, the names often change, the people rotate, but the money pit programs roll on and on until somebody throws the bullshit flag and puts an end to the taxpayer bleeding. I am quite sure that little, if any, tunneler input was ever listened to by the leadership pressing for a program that could not deliver. When programs go "roller political" and the careers of long-term, professional executive bureaucrats are potentially affected by exposure of such ignorance, good decision making goes out the window and the turd shining and tossing reaches biblical proportions.

The dung beetle manager must be prepared to hear the art of the possible that may be contrary to political and senior leadership strategies and goals. More importantly, the dung beetle manager must be able to have the discipline to challenge "facts," and then have the courage of his or her convictions to know when to throw the bullshit flag down hard and say "no" or "not yet." Always ask your tunnelers to provide options and solutions to go with their predisposition to say no. If pressed to do so, the true tunneler can and will give you any number of executable options to work with. A leader's instincts are great, but they are no substitute for the Scotties of the world who know where the red line is on the engine of change. Failure to listen to your tunnelers could cost you a perfectly good leadership opportunity or your job.

CHAPTER 10

THE DWELLERS

Some people actually have fart disorders. And I hear it gets worse as you get older. Shortly after graduating from the university with my Masters Degree in Economics, I went to work in a major regional bank as a federal funds money market trader. I was responsible for placing an average of $1 billion in bank reserves each day at a margin that was at least one-quarter of a percent (or 25 basis points) above the reverse repurchase agreements the bank sold. My boss was a retired female army warrant officer named Kathy. Kathy was an iron balls, no frills, and no fluff kind of lady who was a blast to work with, but you could never really be sure where you stood with her until it was too late.

On one Friday morning, I had taken a long position in fed funds by about $200 million and bought that amount back later in the day for about one hundred and twenty-five basis points less than I sold them for in the morning. I was riding high, expecting to get noticed for my market wizardry and trading skills. This particular weekend was also a holiday weekend, which meant that the profits would accumulate for three days instead of two. A hundred and twenty-five basis points on $200 million for three days was not chump change for earnings. Those were big returns to boost earnings per share, and the bank's shareholders would be proud.

On the Tuesday when we all returned to work, I got a call from the Investment Division manager and Kathy summoned me to join her for the meeting. This was it – my breakthrough as a financial wizard. Just a few weeks on the job and I was in the front office with the big dogs. We walked into the Division manager's office, and he said that the bank president had called him first thing and asked to find out who the trader was who was to be fired that day for making such a mess of his return on average asset numbers for the month. That trader was me. Turns out, return on average assets is of greater value to a conservative regional bank than earnings per share, and my $200 million increase in average assets with the nominal 125 basis point increase in earnings had clobbered our bank's return on average asset figures in the first reporting week of the month. The Division manager relayed the president's message: "Tell that boy he did good for a high-risk Wall Street guy, but this is not Wall Street and if he ever does it again, I'll send him to New York to play loose with other people's money." From that day on, I was restricted to a $40 million position in either the short or long direction and never strayed again.

Kathy's revenge for my own little poorade was subtle but effective. She called me to her office the next day and said, "OK, hot shot, I need you to take that glitz and glamour down to the first deck and escort up one of my high-rent customers."

I asked, "How will I know what he looks like?" Kathy follows up with, "He'll know you by your bullshit and swagger and introduce himself."

So off I went, down to the lobby wondering who the psychic rich guy was who could pick me out of a crowd. This really, really old guy shuffles up to me and says, "You must be Kathy's boy, I could tell by that shit-eating grin and the nametag." I introduced myself to Mr. P and exchanged pleasantries as we headed for the elevator.

As we started that short walk, I noticed that Mr. P was farting every other step. Step-fart, step-fart. He was not subtle about it and did not seem to care that everyone else was picking up on it. As we approached the elevator, I was aghast because it was nearly full of women from up in the credit department. They graciously held the door open for me and Mr. P. We get in and Mr. P does not let up, at least one fart per floor. The farts were those old, loose-ass, wiggly warble farts that almost sounded like wet bubble farts. And they stunk like goat cheese between your toes on a hot summer day. I don't know if you have ever been a victim of an elevator fart attack, but sometimes pinpointing the culprit is a proximity thing. And I happened to be in Mr. P's proximity.

There are four universal responses to a fart. The first is complete passivity. You have seen the people who appear to go out of their way to remain unresponsive to a fart. Their facial expression doesn't change; there are no noticeable movements, and no words. It is as though the fart and farter never existed. The passive response is more likely if the fart doesn't stink. The passive fart observer is a rarity (because most farts stink), but they do exist. The next response is the "annoyed phew." These observers make the stinky face whether there is a smell or not, and grimace for public consumption. Sometimes the annoyed phew are known to make a comment like "Do you mind?," "How dare you," or "Excuse you." The third fart observer is the benevolent giggler. The benevolent giggler turns away from the farter and giggles in low tones so as not to be overheard. Benevolent gigglers tend to be in small groups, and are mostly women or girls. The last type of fart observer is the nut buster. Nut busters tend to be guys, and they simply burst out laughing, almost uncontrollably, when observing a fart in progress or in public. To a nut buster all farts are funny, and they can laugh at farts for hours.

Upon hearing a fart in an elevator, most people make a face and look at the person next to them aghast and animated, as if they care, somewhere in between an annoyed phew and benevolent giggler range of responses. The lookee, fearing designation as the perpetrator, usually engages the looker in the same face-contorting, animated behavior. This goes on in small concentric circles for a while until everyone has "reacted." If you happen to be the one cutting the cheese, and wish to remain anonymous (if it was a silent but deadly type fart), you must engage in the same behavior as those around you. If you don't give a shit, it's just fun to watch.

The elevator stopped on five separate floors and just as the last girl lurched out of the elevator gasping for the air she had been depriving herself of for nine floors, Mr. P looks at me and says, "Well I hope you got that out of your system." So I had been pegged as the elevator fart maniac by Mr. Flatulence himself. As Mr. P and I left the elevator, he continued the step-fart-step-fart rhythm all the way to Kathy's office. I guess the look on my face said it all, and she took Mr. P into her office and they did their big business deal, and I went back to the trading desk in a daze.

Later in the day Kathy walks up to my desk and says, "So Mr. P's a stinker, isn't he?" I turned around and said, "Did you know he practically shit himself all the way up to your office and then blamed me for it!" Kathy said, "Of course, he has chronic flatulence and quite a sense of humor. It's kind of like yesterday when I came into work and got blamed by the Division manager for my subordinate shitting all over the bank's return on average assets." She smiled, patted me on the shoulder, and gracefully walked away.

Dwellers live in the dung pile. They do not risk rolling a ball and heading away from the pile to fight the sideline-loving shit eaters, who wait for someone else to do the dirty work, then try to steal it. Dwellers don't go to the extra effort to dig directly under the dung pile either. There is less work just staying in the fresh, soft stuff. If you are familiar with the statistical bell curve, approximately sixty-eight percent of the population with a normal distribution lies within plus or minus one standard deviation from the mean. The mean, translated for the less mathematically inclined, is the happy place where most of the people center near the average. I don't have the federal- or DoD-level numbers to support this, but the powers of observation and my own experience places around sixty-five to seventy-percent of the workforce in the middle of the performance curve. They are the brilliant ones who fully grasp that whether we have a five-point scale, pass/fail, or the National Security Personnel System (also referred to as NSPS or NSBS by some who have worked in it long enough) performance plan, the system always tends to work its way into a forced distribution. So if you don't have a sugar daddy or momma who will shower you with high performance marks, odds are you will melt into the center of the curve regardless of how hard you work or what you contribute. Given that likelihood and the unkind tradeoff between quality of life and the extra five to six thousand dollars per year you might get if you work an extra ten to twenty hours a week and often on weekends, the dweller mind is quick to do the math and burrow into the soft center of the pile.

Dwellers compose the majority of the workforce, and they provide the majority of the work and product. Dwellers operate at a comfortable, steady state mode, and give little above the minimum effort necessary to do the work. And why should they? They see rollers getting knocked around, rising and falling, and leading unbalanced lives and logically conclude that's nuts. They see tunnelers putting extra brain power and attention to detail for that little extra margin of excellence only to be normalized into the center of the performance curve and demoralized of their dreams of making a difference in the federal universe. You don't want to be blocking the office exits near the end of the normal workday, nor wandering aimlessly in the parking lots when the dwellers complete their standard eight hour day. They will stampede you in the exits and leave skid marks when they get in their cars. The job is a means unto an end, and the dweller will tend to be the one who is coaching little league, doing volunteer work, or some fulfilling hobby or life interest that is totally unrelated to their jobs.

Dwellers also tend to be active in labor unions because of their experience in the middle of the bell curve and desire to fight for equity in distribution of raises, bonuses, perks, or other items that impact the steady state job they have to perform for supervisory and management "idiots" who just don't get it. It is a self-fulfilling prophecy that dwellers find themselves in the middle of a bell curve while fighting hard for equity in distribution of the goodies. Anyone who thinks lowly of those who anchor the masses and center of the productivity curve is wrong to do so. All things trend toward an equilibrium state, and all things are continually agitated and disrupted while trying to do so. One of the things I loved about being an economist was that we would begin all arguments with "other things being equal." That was necessary to theoretically and practically isolate effects, but in reality, nothing is in steady state for very long. As a central theme to this book, shit happens a lot from a lot of different places all the time. Dwellers maintain critical continuity and hold the steady state bar up for the rollers and tunnelers. Dwellers know the business and have seen hundreds of attempts to execute total quality leadership, rapid improvement, continuous improvement events, and any number of other elephant brain farts that were attempted in the name of innovation and progress. Dwellers are a skeptical lot, and for good reason. Dwellers are the main obstacle to change, yet one of the most powerful agents for change if properly engaged and managed.

If you want to get the dwellers into the change game, you have to let them unleash their frustrations and skepticism right up front, then work with them to establish pilot or prototype efforts to test under very controlled conditions. Once a dweller team makes a breakthrough on a new process or method, they will inspire others and become strong advocates to expand the improvement throughout the organization. If dwellers perceive any likelihood of failure or risk in taking on a change, they will simply and effectively wait out the leadership pushing the issue. Dwellers are much more patient than the leadership that is trying to change their daily lives.

Since dwellers have power in numbers, tunnelers have power in precision and process, and rollers have power in vision and energy; the dung beetle triangle is complete only with all three working in harmony. If dwellers did not exist, rollers and tunnelers could not clear the dung pile fast enough and the world would become encrusted in shit. The dung beetle population would eventually die off since the rollers and tunnelers are not as efficient in the basics of the shit-eating circle of life. Without rollers and tunnelers churning up the ground, the long-term aeration and moisturizing effects of the cleanup work would diminish and the ground would foul. Foul ground means less nutrients, less grass, more disease, and fewer shitters. Fewer shitters mean less fuel for the dung beetle circle of life. If you have watched the United States auto industry, you can see the long-term negative effects of excessive dweller influence. Since the Great Depression, the U.S. auto industry has lobbied for protection from foreign competition in the U.S., citing unfair competition and maintenance of the status quo for jobs and communities. Chrysler was bailed out by the federal government in the 1980s, and the massive bailout efforts of 2009 were argued on similar merits. The argument has always gone that we need more time and investment in new technology to get ahead of the foreign automakers, and meanwhile negotiate for inordinate salaries for blue-collar skill workers and income guarantees and severance packages that almost no company could afford. And at the executive levels, there has been little or no regard for the need for fuel efficiency, nor concern for the communities and the people who make the product. The ground is now fouling for the U.S. auto industry, and the status quo will never be what it was for many employees and communities.

My brother Tony told me a good dweller story. Tony works in the asphalt industry, and one day he was called out to a job to resolve a mechanical problem with the paving equipment. The equipment had been down for several hours by the time he arrived and successfully resolved the issue. Tony directed the crew to get back to work but they refused, citing their right to their mandatory breaks and lunch period. None of them had considered the possibility of grabbing some chow while kicked back in the shade for almost three hours drinking soda, water, and smoking. So my impatient little brother jumps up on the paving machine and takes off, fully intending to get the job back on schedule. The crew finally concedes to get back in the game since he would have moved the equipment quite a distance down the road, and asphalt is really hot, especially when it is laid down in the middle of the summer heat. Upon returning to his office, he was reprimanded since the local union steward had heard of his infraction in logic and filed an unfair labor practice against him and the company for trying to force the road crew to work on their lunch break.

The major downside to the core dweller mentality is that long-term productivity and cost control are not generally primary considerations for their day job. Performing the job and serving customers is a routine part of the day, and any actions attempting to change the status quo are met with intense, emotional reactions. In more extreme cases, change is met with unionization attempts, unfair labor practice claim volumes that choke off management's time for strategic and tactical planning, and work stoppages.

If you have ever gone into an office that provides entitlement program administration (e.g., Social Security, Medicare, Medicaid) you can see dweller attitudes prevail all over those organizations because of the high volume of transformational, house cleaning, or other shake-up attempts that are cycled through them with each political cycle. I have observed strong positive correlation between dwellers trying to assume control and the volume of churn and change lobbed at an organization. When this occurs, organizations encrust and become increasingly irrelevant and unresponsive to the changing world around them. This dweller encrustation may seem like a near-term course for stability, but invariably fouls the ground for the long-term future of any organization. Rollers and tunnelers should understand their contribution to this dynamic and always pace change in a way that embraces the dweller workforce instead of taking a negative, confrontational approach to driving change.

CHAPTER 11

THE TRAVELING DUNG BEETLE

The strangest flight I ever have experienced was with my old buddy Rick (the deranged PhD). We were on a U.S. Airways Boeing 727 flight from Washington, D.C., to Orlando, FL. Rick and I were working on a project to evaluate having contractors provide Navy E-6A (a big 707 derivative aircraft that flies in big circles with an antenna that trails it so we can talk to submarines) instead of doing it with an organic navy organization with the associated overhead and military culture. We had become well versed in most of the training curriculum and had learned many of the procedures for heavy aircraft. The flight was routine, and over the years I had gotten accustomed to the usual bit of turbulence that is normal when jets cross the jet stream somewhere along the mid-Atlantic coast.

Rick and I were in the back row seats (shit smellers) on this flight; I was in the aisle and he was at the window seat. The skies were a magnificent blue and spotted with the occasional puffy white cloud. We had been airborne for about an hour and were somewhere near North Carolina when the jet stream turbulence began. The typical experience was some light bouncing in the vertical axis and that was it. This time we noticed the aircraft bouncing in the vertical and horizontal axes, which was a bit more severe than normal. As the pilot started to correct for the yaw and roll, we noticed the aircraft beginning to oscillate, yaw, and roll almost to the limits of the aircraft design. Imagine flying along at an altitude of thirty-two thousand feet going five hundred miles per hour with your wings dipping right, then left, over a wide arc while the nose is oscillating from left to right. We were pretty sure anything greater than forty-five degrees of roll from straight and normal flight was getting into a place we did not want to be. The term for this peculiar combination of oscillations is a Dutch Roll. It happens in very thin air when an aircraft gets a severe yaw and roll combination, and it is very difficult to regain control of the aircraft.

The one thing Rick and I were both sure of was that this airplane was about to do a very quick and steep dive down into thick air so the pilot could regain control. That was one of the emergency procedures we had learned for the Dutch Roll. Just as the pilot pushed the controls forward, driving the aircraft sharply down, a flight attendant had gotten next to my seat and was suddenly lifted off her feet and floating in the air while holding on to the arm of my seat. There were books, apples, trays, cups, and all manner of junk floating in the air with some shrieking and screaming. The flight attendant was suspended in this moon float position for about fifteen seconds until the pilot gently leveled off and the earth's suckage (aka gravity) pulled her and all the junk down with a thud and various crashing noises.

After we received the "all clear" sign from the flight attendants, Rick needed to go to the head (bathroom) and either clean his pants or take a piss. I got up out of my seat to let him by and he walked back to the head, opened the door, paused a moment, then closed it. He turned to the moon-walking flight attendant and said, "There's somebody in there that looks like she's in shock, and I think you'd better help her. It looks like Tipper Gore's (Senator and Vice President Al Gore's wife) stuck on the can with her white stockings around her ankles."

And it was. Mrs. Gore had been in the can for the moonwalk and had to be as surprised as some of the rest of us. Only she had not had the benefit of a seatbelt at the time and had taken Mr. Toad's Wild Ride in the airplane potty that day. She collected herself and went on doing fundraisers and appearances in the Central Florida area, and we never mentioned it or heard about it again. So, Tipper, if you read this, I am sure you'll never forget that flight, and it was my buddy Rick who walked in on you. He did not take any pictures that I am aware of.

In my travels I have been puked on, had a 10-year-old kid shit his pants sitting next to me – no less than three times during a 5 ½ hour flight – had a 10-pound bag dropped on my head that broke the skin and caused bleeding, had hot coffee poured on my crotch, causing second-degree burns on my special purpose (thanks to that unknown stupid woman who kept flipping the newspaper fully open and knocked my coffee into my lap), had the old Dutch Roll, complained about air blowing in from the emergency exit on a US Airways plane that broke apart the next day when landing in Pensacola, FL, experienced a two thousand foot drop from wind sheer on a puddle hopper over Texas that put an 80-year-old first-time lady flier in my lap, had a dog shit in his cage and half the plane blamed me for it (dog was behind the wall in the last row of a puddle hopper behind me), sat next to some of the most seat-width-challenged Americans God has placed on this planet and had to smell their armpits for hours, sat next to a Hari Krishna that hadn't seen soap or water in a decade whose funk had people puking around us, blew out an eardrum due to a blockage in my ear, and have sat next to more uncontrolled, unaccompanied minors than I wish to count. This entire lengthy chapter is devoted to providing travel advice to all dung beetle managers, the work force, and traveling public because we all share the same air up there.

I have a lot of traveling pet peeves and can recall the good old days before airline deregulation when most flights were no more than half full, you got real meals on flights with real utensils, and most flight attendants were actually happy you were on their flight. The downside to flying during those days was the smoking section. It was very similar to the invisible line between smoking and nonsmoking tables in restaurants that still cater to smokers. If you happened to be within five rows of the smoking section in those days, you might as well have pulled the filter off a Camel and went at it. These days, the last five rows of the aircraft have replaced the smell of cigarettes with the smell of toilets. If the flight is over an hour long, you can expect to see the teeny-weenie bladder club all lined up with their butts stuck in the face of the poor schmucks in the aisle seats. And to add insult to injury, the number two assholes stand there in the aisle squeaking off SBD (silent but deadly) farts.

The enterprising Dung Beetle manager will apply good logic to keeping the butts of dozens of strangers out of their faces by avoiding boarding airplanes quickly when you have an aisle seat. The only time getting on fast is important is when you are trying to carry on two bags and need the overhead space. So if you are a two-bagger, you trade off overhead space with butts in your face.

As a general rule, if your butt touches both armrests when you sit down, it will also encroach into the seat next to you. And your shoulders tend to be wider than your butt, so you do the math. I for one advocate that airlines, with the full faith and support of the federal government, make people who are a couple of standard deviations larger than the average seat width pay a premium for multiple seat encroachment on airplanes. They do it for luggage. You've seen the little frame mock-up out in the gate area that says, "If your bag won't fit in this space, you must check it." There needs to be a seat out there that says, "If your ass won't fit in this, you must pay for two seats or ride with your luggage." Even today, any bag over 50 pounds is "excessive" weight and you get charged a premium. You take an extra bag, and you get charged a premium. You show up 100 pounds overweight, and I get to sit next to your stinky armpits rubbing asses with you all the way to Reagan National Airport. It's not fair and needs to change. Call your freshman congressman and senators and send a lot of e-mail to the airlines. It won't change anything, but you'll feel like you are doing something about the injustice of sharing your seat and subsidizing the fuel bill for the guy or girl in the seat next to you. If you find yourself in this situation, it will most likely be a full flight and you can ask to be reseated, but don't expect anyone on the airplane to give a damn. They don't. If it is not a full flight, as soon as the "fasten seat belt sign" goes off, get up and find another seat. Take your bag with you, inadvertently slip and push your ass into the face of the large person if they are between you and the aisle and they refuse to get up and let you out. They'll get pissed and want to fight or become visibly irritated and will not attempt to understand their encroachment on your space since they are accustomed to taking up extra room on airplanes and expect you to take it in the name of democracy. If they hit you, they get arrested by the air marshal and taken to jail upon landing so you have that going for you. Another technique I have tried during armpit overload was to request premature release of the overhead oxygen mask. The airlines don't like to set a precedent that way, so the answer is always no on that one.

Airport security since 9-11 has been a trip. Every airport and airline is a little different. When I travel, I usually carry my Florida Driver's License, other federal identification cards, and the now defunct Clear National Traveler Program Card. To get the Clear card, you had to submit to a national screening and your image and biometric data (iris scan or fingerprint) was loaded onto a computer chip on the card and national database. Given all of the above, I still get flagged for "extra or special" screening on the occasional one-way or quickly booked trip. Usually, the airline you fly will waive off the "extra" screening if you are a frequent traveler, have Government ID or Clear card, but some are just pricks. If I am outbound with clean clothes in my bag, I always unravel my underwear and lay them on top just in case I get the "hands on" treatment. If I am coming home with a lot of dirty underwear, those always go on top for the gloved ones at TSA to sort through for those special times.

For the first six months after 9-11, I had my groin touched by no less than a dozen TSA agents during the "extra" screening. Some men, some women, and some I'm not so sure of. They never found anything interesting down there, but it seemed to be a popular place to touch during searches. One of my friends is a pilot with United Airlines and said that while he was authorized to have a gun in the cockpit of the airplane, along with the crash axe that is in there, he could not get through security with a plastic knife and fork. He figured that even if they did not let him have his knife and fork, he could still stir up some real shit on the plane using the gun or axe in the cockpit if he wanted to. Too bad airline pilots cannot eat rice noodles with a crash axe.

Now about those people who cannot seem to control their bladders and bowels on a plane. I'd estimate that about fifty percent of the time when I am in the aisle seat on a flight lasting at least one hour, one of the people between me and the window gets up to take a piss or dump as soon as the plane gets to cruising altitude. Come on, America. The average bladder can handle a couple of hours of pee and, short of diarrhea, you can hold a turd back for a couple of hours. Better yet, take that pre-flight piss or dump and save us all the joy of pulling down the tray, getting out the computer, hooking up the headset, and getting the drink only to have your dumb ass make us reel it all back in to let you out to go to the potty. And if you happen to be unfortunate enough to sit in the last five rows on the aisle, you will have anywhere from twenty to forty minutes of butts in your face, with at least some of them squeezing off a fart here and there as they hold back the pressure on the old bunghole. I do not ever recommend sitting anywhere in the last five rows for any flight lasting longer than one hour. If you find yourself there on an international flight, God help you, and take some Vicks Vapor Rub and be prepared to put it on your nose.

On those rare occasions when I have had to go to the potty on an airplane and do a number two, I have found a great way to minimize my environmental impact to the rest of the crew and passengers. Upon planting your backside on the seat (or hovering as the case may be), as soon as you drop the load hit the flush button. On the newer aircraft, there is a tornado sucking sound as half the air in the little room gets pulled out with whatever you left in the hole. Whoever came up with that mechanism needs an award. On the older aircraft, you still have the old port-o-let blue funk that doesn't do a great job of sucking out the smell. On those aircraft, speed and timing are of the essence. Start the flush the moment before the release. Multiple flushes are usually necessary to complete the process in either case. Once you are done, you get to wash one hand at a time with those stupid sinks that require you to hold down the water valve to make it work. And guys, if you are taking a piss, for the sake of all the women and people who might need to take a dump on the plane, put the damn seat up. If you are afraid to touch it, unroll some toilet paper, put it in your hand, and use that to lift the seat. If you are one of the number two crowd and fail to follow my instructions, may the people on the last five rows have their way with you, along with the person in line behind you. You can rest assured; there is no doubt who did what on an airplane potty. It's kind of like farting in a large elevator – the suspect list is short and manageable.

Another safety tip for airline passengers: beware of the chair launchers. These are the idiots who grab the back of your seat (and sometimes your hair) to pull themselves up, then abruptly let go and send your brain stem through your teeth. The moment you feel someone grab the back of your seat and pull, lean forward until they release it. If they pull your hair, I recommend getting on your knees and turning around in your seat and staring at the perpetrator. They always act like you are the weird guy or girl, and sometimes I even smile and say, "Hello, my brain stem is now in my teeth, thanks for helping me floss."

Amateur drummers and kids fall into the next category of risk for the weary traveler. Based on the laws of physics and the fact that your tray is connected to the back of someone else's seat, any force exerted on the tray is felt in the seat and brain of the person in front of you. For all you amateur drummers or parents who travel with kids, that means when you or the kids pound out a riff on the tray table, you are causing high-frequency brain oscillations and risking brain explosions for the people seated in front of you. Don't be an idiot, and don't pound on the tray tables. If you happen to have an idiot or innocent child behind you doing Wipe Out, get up on your knees, turn around, smile at them, and say, "I like my brain, please stop or I may throw up," and keep staring until they quit or the kid's parents get a clue. If you are the parent of a kid, don't be an idiot and keep your kids from pounding on the tray tables.

Brain damage is possible on airplanes, especially now with most of the airlines charging fifteen to twenty-five bucks to check a bag. Everybody now wants to carry on their luggage, and the competition for overhead space is high. As noted earlier, if you are a two bagger, you have to get on a full plane within the first two-thirds of the passenger load or plan to leave your bag at the end of the jet way to be checked. Don't be one of those ass wipes who is the last guy on a full plane who brings on the extra bag. It is not now nor ever in your future going to fit. All the spaces are full, dumbass. So don't drag a large suitcase down the aisle, knocking all of the aisle-seated passengers in the arm or head with your bag, only to get pissed off and drag it out while cursing under your breath and hit us again. If you happen to be seated in the aisle, be very attentive of what is going on around your head. I have been hit in the head more times than I can remember by all manner of humans swinging their luggage up and down from the overhead bins. Maybe that's why I cannot remember too well these days. One darling lady in Atlanta dropped her solid ten-pound purse on my head and it broke the skin and began to bleed. When I mentioned it to the flight attendant on the airline I now refer to as "the airline I will never fly again in this or any future life", she looked at my head and decided it was not significant enough for stitches, and laughed that I must have a hard head. She wouldn't even bring me a wash rag to wipe off the blood. I mentioned it to the lead flight attendant as I was getting off the plane, and he concluded it could not have been too bad if it had already clotted, my pupils were not dilated, and I was not babbling. After two other miserable flights with that particular airline, I gave up trying to resolve problems with them. The other risk of sitting in the aisle comes when you stand up and are leaning just to one side or the other and the nimrod behind you opens the overhead bin and the door flies open and hits you in the head.

The other rules for aisle sitters are as follows: (1) If there is an empty seat beside you, never buckle your seatbelt until the door is shut and everybody has boarded. Otherwise you'll get all cozy and the person in that seat will want to get in. Get up, let them in, then sit down and buckle up. If you don't, you will get your feet stepped on, have a butt or worse in your face, and deserve it since you did not get up and let the person in; (2) during the boarding process, keep your elbow off the aisle side armrest and lean toward the window. If you fail to follow this guidance, your elbow will get hit numerous times and you may get a hair muff from an ass rubbing into your head; and (3) beware of the skinny area under the seat in front of you for storing your bag. Many aisle seats have smaller storage areas below the seat in front of you, and if you have a standard computer bag, it most likely will not fit. If you get stuck with a bag that is too large to fit, and there is no more overhead space, your precious computer may get tossed into the luggage bin due to FAA regulations on foot clearance for under-seat storage. I've seen it happen.

When boarding an aircraft, focus on the two "B's" – butt and bags – and be aware of where your butt and bags are at all times. I am always amazed and pissed off by the volume of people who plod down the aisle banging their ass into people and swinging their bags around without any regard for the people sitting on the plane. The backpack and purse carriers are the worst. When they turn, they have an additional foot or so of luggage hanging on their anatomy that always hits someone. If you are carrying a backpack or purse, take them off or walk straight. And for those of you who want to roll your bag down the aisle, do it with great caution because you will have about an inch of clearance on either side without legs and elbows protruding into the aisle, and also have seatbelts hanging down to catch your bag as you roll through. My knees and elbows know who you are.

There should be a law against farting on an airplane. Even though dung beetles should be conditioned to foul air, the air in an aircraft is a closed system, and it takes a long time for the stench-to-air molecule ratio to get to a point where the average nose cannot pick up on the odor. I have suffered through numerous flights with someone within a ten-row range on either side cutting the cheese. There is nothing you can do to escape it other than to take the Vapor Rub and put it under your nose. Fart detectors in the seats would be awesome so we could identify and fine the hell out of the guilty. We fine people for smoking on airplanes but have no recourse for those emitting flammable and noxious fumes that erode the ozone layer.

When sitting next to a child wearing a red-striped name tag, beware. These are called unaccompanied minors, aka "random time bombs." When they start misbehaving, the people in front or behind you won't know it isn't your kid and will get up on their knees and stare at you when the kid starts pounding on the seat tray, kicking the seat in front of them, or turning the volume up on their video game so loud it has the same effect as military psychological operations with loud, bad music. If an unaccompanied minor pukes, many flight attendants will hand you the rags to clean them up if you don't quickly advise them of the obvious. During a flight from San Diego to Dallas, I sat next to two boys, aged six (Bobby) and eight (Mikey). They were traveling to New York City to see their dad. They were all alone, with their red-striped stickers and me. I was sitting in the window seat, Mikey in the middle, and Bobby on the aisle. The boys were cute as hell, but I knew I was in trouble when Mikey pulled out a teddy bear and says, "You know what I do when Teddy is a bad boy?" I shook my head no and he proceeded to beat the hell out of the teddy bear on the back of the seat in front of me, smacking the occupant in the head many times. The guy in the seat up front turns around on his knees and stares at me. I explained that they were not mine and he did not care and wanted me to restrain the monkeys. So I told Mikey, "This nice man in front of you is going to whip your ass if you do that again." Teddy went under the seat.

The flight attendant, who was wearing a skirt, came up to Bobby and said, "Here's my two pilots," and hands them their wings (with pins). To all the flight attendants out there, that is a bad idea for two boys under the age of ten traveling alone at the beginning of a flight. Bobby kept getting up and running into the aisle and getting under the flight attendant's skirt. She would put him back in his seat and he would say, "I saw her butt! I saw her butt!" To all the flight attendants out there wearing skirts, don't wear butt floss or all the little Bobbies out there might sneak a peak at your ass. The frazzled flight attendant put Bobby back in his seat for the fourth or fifth time and gave me the "God help me" face. I leaned over to Bobby and said, "That nice lady is going to whip your ass if you do that again." Bobby sulked into his seat and started playing with his new aviator wings. Finding the sharp pin, he thought it would be cool to poke his brother's leg with it. Being fair-minded with a bent for reciprocity, Mikey poked him back with his pin. This went on for a couple of minutes with only minor bleeding. I finally had enough and said, "I am going to whip both of your asses if you don't behave the rest of this flight." Things calmed down a bit more after that.

My other unaccompanied minor experience was equally exciting. I was on a small regional jet that ran between Pensacola and Orlando, Florida. There were three seats on the right side, and two on the left. I was in the window seat on the right side, and this adorable little six-year-old girl was in the middle seat between me and another guy. She did not have on the telltale red-striped sticker, so I thought she was traveling with the other guy. He thought she was traveling with me. Only the flight attendant knew the truth and she wasn't talking. Little Molly had curly blond hair and blue eyes. I remember her well because she reminded me of my daughters when they were that age. This flight occurred during the days when you actually got all-you-can-eat peanuts, crackers, cookies, and soda, and Molly was munching down on all the goodies the flight attendant kept giving her. Molly told me about her cat and her dolls and was a charming little angel. Just as we were about to begin our initial descent, Molly looked up at me and said, "My tummy don't feel good and…." No other words made it out. Molly had turned her head back straight and began projectile vomiting with a velocity that sprayed in between the seat backs in front of us, onto the seat backs two rows up. I looked over at the guy sitting next to Molly, and he was looking back at me, and the people in front of us were all up on their knees looking at all of us. The other guy said, "She's not mine," and I said, "Me neither." The flight attendant came running up and said, "Oh my God, I cannot stand the smell of vomit," and ran off. She came running back with a box of wet washrags and the other guy said, "No way, lady, I did not sign on for this." He got up and walked to the back of the aircraft. The two people in front of us started gagging and hurled into their barf bags. At this point, the entire middle section of the aircraft smelled like peanut-laced Coca Cola hurl. The flight attendant was standing there with a bag of rags, gagging and pleading for me to help. I took the box and began cleaning up little Molly and the surrounding area. I only took an incidental splash on my left leg so the direct hurl impact on me was minimal. We went through two boxes of washrags before we got down to cloth and skin. The flight attendant brought me an entire tray of the tiny liquor bottles and told me to have all I wanted. I only took about ten or twenty bottles. After we got off the plane, little Molly's mom heard about the hurl fest and was very grateful somebody had stepped in to help her baby.

The motto of the unaccompanied minor experience is that if you travel enough, some day you may find yourself in the substitute parent role on an airplane. I cannot tell you what to do if it happens, but if you don't step up and intervene, the flight could be a lot worse for a lot of people. Not to mention some precious child whose parents were too cheap, stubborn, or stupid to ride with their own kids. For the parents who think about sending their kids off on an airplane ride unaccompanied, don't be idiots. Care enough about your children and the hundred other passengers for one of you to ride the damn plane.

I am all for religious freedom in America, but I draw the line when Hari Krishnas and others who don't believe in bathing get on an airplane within five rows of me. If I went out and rolled in dog shit, then got on an airplane, I am sure somebody would ask me to get off the aircraft. If I don't clean my ass and go crusty for a month in the name of religious freedom, then get on a plane and people complain, they are messing with my civil rights. I was on another flight between San Diego and Houston when a Hari Krishna sat down in the window seat in the row I was on. I was in the aisle seat and fortunately had my seat belt off and got up before his stinky ass passed in front of me. The funk coming off this guy was palpable and unbelievable. Imagine how your armpits, toe jam, and crotch would smell after about a month without washing, and that was this guy in spades. As the seats started filling around us people were holding their noses, making elevator fart faces, and gestures to their neighbors. Some were talking to the flight attendant asking if they could get this guy off the plane. They were told this was not possible since it was a religion thing. His departure was not in our American rulebook, so we were stunk up by Hairless Krust-ass for the duration. Fortunately there were enough seats around the airplane to eventually clear out about two rows on either side of this guy, but the funk hung around for the whole flight. I ran home and showered but smelled this guy for two more days as my sinuses unclogged and started clearing. I've only had a few other stinkers like this guy, but he took the prize. I complained to the airline, but they assured me there was nothing they could do about it. If you find yourself in a similar situation, talk to the flight attendant immediately, and if it is as bad as old Hairless Krust-ass, I'd recommend asking to take another flight if your schedule permits. Sitting next to him had the same effect as going into a smoke-filled bar. Your sinuses and clothes reek for days and weeks afterward. If you are planning to get on an airplane smelling like an elephant's ass, don't be an idiot. Take a shower or drive your own stinky behind to wherever you are going.

For all of you newspaper readers on airplanes, I give you a word of caution. Fold the damn thing up in quarters and read it that way or leave it in the gate area. I was seated in a window seat on a small regional jet one morning headed to Pensacola from Orlando. We had just hit cruising altitude and the flight attendants were coming through the cabin with coffee. I had just received my coffee, and the lady sitting next to me whipped out her *USA Today* and opened it full width. She did the full-spread flip, where you thumb the next page then snap the paper and it maintains the fold in half. There was ample room to not infringe on my space, but that did not seem to deter this woman. I moved my coffee to the right side of my tray to avoid her paper flailing. Then on the next flip, she did not get the sharp fold and the paper hung up halfway. She snapped it again with such a force it hit my tray and knocked my fresh, hot coffee into my crotch. The pain was incredible. When heat cannot escape, it simply goes where it has to in order to equalize temperatures. In this case, it went onto my nuts and scorched second-degree burns into them. So here I am in incredible pain, and this stupid lady who knocked off my coffee is nervously laughing at the situation. Her only words on the subject were "Oh my, was that hot?" The flight attendant heard me cursing and moving around and asked what she could do to help. Short of me dropping my pants right there and asking someone to ice my nuts, I asked her for cold wash rags. After cooling the jewels down, I went into the head and examined the damage. It was sufficient to warrant a large ball of toilet paper to minimize skin to cloth contact. Upon landing, I appeared quite well endowed with the toilet paper ball in my pants and proceeded straight to the infirmary and received treatment that included gauze, antibiotics, and burn cream. The real bitch of it was that I only had one pair of pants for the two-day trip. Fortunately, the pants were black and the coffee stain was not noticeable, but I smelled like old coffee with scorched nuts and had to sit through a day of meetings with gauze, burn cream, cream and sugar, and coffee. I did not even consider filing a lawsuit against the airline for having hot coffee. Where I grew up, coffee is supposed to be hot and they teach you that in elementary school. The lady who knocked the coffee off my tray did not mean to do it; she was just a moron. So the moral of this lesson is to leave your newspapers in the gate area or be excruciatingly careful when you try to change pages on a plane. And if you find yourself sitting next to or in front of a dumbass that is wildly flipping a paper around, immediately grab the paper and put an end to it. It is not necessary and just irritating to everybody around you. If you happen to be an avid paper reader, don't be an idiot – read it before or after the flight.

I have given up on using a laptop on airplanes. The designers of laptops strategically sized the screens so that when you place the computer on the tray, and the person in front of you reclines his or her seat all the way back in the sudden, spastic way so many people do, then the tray latch or inset where the tray is stored will catch the top of the display screen and break it. I witnessed several broken screens before I started keeping mine pointed slightly toward me. While this reduces the risk of screen breakage, it makes it very hard to read. When you combine this with the boneheads sitting next to you who wait until you get all set up with a computer and a drink to decide it's time to take a piss, it's just not worth the trouble. There's also the problem of solar angles when someone leaves a window open and the sun shines directly into it onto your screen. You can't see a damn thing. Get a good book, listen to your MP3 player, or sleep. Leave the computer in the bag unless you really, really have to work on the plane. If you are using a portable DVD player, beware of the same problems.

I have only had my luggage lost five times in twenty-four years of heavy traveling so as traumatic as it can be, it does not happen as often as some would believe. For the dung beetle manager who has to plan to be in a suit or business attire upon arrival, I recommend wearing one complete business suit on your outbound trip. This is from the personal experience of having had my luggage go to Mexico while I was going to San Diego. Upon arrival, I had no business attire to wear and did not feel like spending three to four hundred dollars to solve the problem for one day. When my luggage did arrive, I was elated, then shocked into the reality that I had packed no belt, but had packed one cordovan left shoe and one black left shoe. Tennis shoes and a suit looks weird, even in California. Now, I always wear a complete business suit on the way out and never worry if my luggage fails to make it in a day or two.

Weather can be forecast in general terms, but it is very unpredictable in specific terms. When flying just about anywhere in the Southeastern United States in the summer, you can expect frequent weather delays. Another summer fact of life is the "thermal bounce" that you get when the aircraft gets below ten thousand feet during takeoff and landing. For the infrequent traveler, this can be very disturbing. There are a few major weather events that just mess up everything and they are hurricanes, massive storm fronts, and snowstorms. If your travel plans get tangled up in one of these events, plan to be rerouted to as many as three or four hops to get where you want to go, or plan to stick around for a couple of days. God is God, and we don't get a vote on where "acts of God" occur. This is important for those of you who wish to stand in the special service line and spend hours bitching about the poor men and women working to reroute or minimize the grief to each customer they see. It takes ten to twenty minutes per customer to work those issues, so those lines are going to move slowly. No matter how much you complain about it, it won't change weather delay reality. The only real complaint I have about airlines and weather is when a storm front is approaching an airport and the traveling public gets caught up in on-time departure statistical buffoonery. The airplane proceeds to exit the gate for an "on-time" departure and then sits on the tarmac for two to four hours while the storm blows through. Then we get to sit another hour while the northeast corridor air-traffic controllers untangle the mountains of aircraft stacked up along the eastern seaboard. Then we find out we sat too long idling the engines and need more fuel. It would be really cool if we did not have to get on the plane at all in those circumstances until the FAA ground holds have cleared and traffic is flowing again. When the interminable ground hold occurs, always remember that the flight attendants did not make the decision so those who like to hold somebody responsible and share their true feelings, save it for the pilot and airline operations team.

Another annoying behavior in airports is what I refer to as camping in the traffic lanes. These human traffic jams occur everywhere in jet ways, at gate exits, and in the main terminal where people now wait for arriving passengers. Imagine driving down the road and having five to ten cars just decide to park in the intersection and start shooting the shit. If you live in Boston, you don't have to imagine it since random parking in traffic lanes appears to be normal around Bean Town. You'd be dreaming of car missiles to take them out, and you get the same sensation when walking out of a jet way and having the terminally ignorant decide to stop at the door and do their hair, make phone calls, put on makeup, or start striking up conversation with the really neat person they just met on the plane. Get your dumb ass out of the hammer lane and go talk where people are not trying to walk. A worse scenario is when a large family is gathered at the main terminal waiting on their long lost relative and decides to do a group grope in the twelve-to-twenty-foot choke point where all passenger traffic exits. Campers show up every time I fly, and I have not found an effective way to mitigate this without becoming a complete and total asshole.

There is a class of traveler you need to be aware of and be prepared to encounter. They can easily be spotted by their eyes and look on their faces. They are the confused, anxious, and infrequent travelers that I refer to as the "terminally confused." Their eyes have a look of fear and anxiety, generally wide, with eyebrows raised high as if they are in a high state of alert and confusion. I associate the look to a prairie dog that senses something moving out in the distance. These people move suddenly and make frequent, random directional changes for no apparent reason. You might think they are taking evasive maneuvers, but the behavior is driven by a simple fear of the unknown location of the gate, the toilet, the restaurant, phones, or automated teller machine. They bump into each other and the rest of us, never seeming to notice how pissed off we get when they cut our feet out from under us with their roller bags, and cut into every line imaginable and think it is OK since they didn't know where they were at. If you watch people's faces, you can see them and execute an early avoidance maneuver and stay clear of them. Otherwise, control your anger when they start bouncing into you and tripping you.

And then there is the guy or girl who is on their cell phone talking so loud everyone within twenty feet can hear every word. The real winners in this group are the people who do it to try and impress you with their command of industry, the split-second, life-altering decisions of a salesman on the road, or the long lost lover who has hotness oozing off his or her chest. I was in a toilet one day and heard a voice say, "Hello, hello," then a pause, then "Can anybody hear me?" Of course, I was concerned that the guy could have been sitting on the shitter having a coronary so I said, "Hey, are you all right?."

The response was "Hello?"

I ask again, "Are you OK, do you need help?"

Answer, "No, no, it's not good."

As I exit my stall, I say, "I'm going to call for assistance."

Answer, "Yes, the parts arrived this week but the son of a bitch installer never showed."

At this point it was obvious that I had just had a parallel universe communication experience with someone who thought I was talking to someone else. I have had numerous occasions where people begin talking on their phones loudly and cannot decipher if I am the target of their conversation or not. The obvious solution is to avoid responding to all stray communication, but then your friends, family, and colleagues traveling with you think you are going deaf since you never respond to them.

When you park a vehicle, write down where you parked it and on which side of which terminal. I have "lost" my truck and several rental cars as a result of not doing this. My best car loss was in Philadelphia. I had parked my white Ford Taurus rental car at the terminal there since I had to go to Washington, DC. The next day I returned with an extra fifty pounds of electronic equipment and proceeded smartly to my car. In the Philly airport, there are seven parking garages (A through F) including an A-east and an A-west to keep things simple. I had parked in the A-west lot, but had left in the C terminal and returned in the B terminal. Having failed to recognize how many parking garages there were, I thought I had parked in the B garage. You would be amazed at how many white Ford Taurus rental cars find their way into Philadelphia airport parking garages. I searched several floors dragging a suitcase, computer bag, and three boxes of equipment, attempted to open no less than five white Ford Taurus rental cars, and finally stopped to ask a security officer on a golf cart for assistance. I told him that I thought my car may have been stolen and he laughed. Exhausted from dragging around all of the equipment, I asked him if he could give me a ride and help me find my car. He said, "They don't pay me enough to drive around every idiot who loses their car in this airport," and drove away laughing his ass off. I finally dropped my luggage off with the concierge at the airport Marriott and then set off on a two-hour journey at 2100 hours to find that damn white Ford Taurus. I spent the next two hours going through every parking garage walking on every level, hitting the panic button, trying at every white Ford Taurus to find the car. I finally did find that white Ford Taurus and drove my sweaty ass wearing a suit to the Marriott, retrieved my bags, and headed on out to Jersey. So if you are unfamiliar with an airport parking garage arrangement, write down where you park and keep it with you. If you are in a rental car and in a strange airport, write down where you park and avoid renting a white Ford Taurus. I'd go with something yellow or green.

Hotels are an entirely different travel focus area. I can keep this discussion short and to the point. If you travel a lot, it is in your interest to choose the same hotel chain as often as possible. I have woken up too many nights in different hotels to find myself disoriented and walking into walls, entering closets for bathrooms, and have had my share of backaches from the variety of really shitty beds out there. When choosing a hotel chain, pick the one that has the best beds. The rest of the amenities are not that significant, and the hotels with the best beds tend to have the better stuff anyway. There is one other tip you need to be aware of. Hotels have recently started hiding the hair dryers in the closets or below the sinks where they are not that easy to spot. After spending half an hour one morning searching for the hair dryer, I called the front desk and asked what the deal was with the "hide and seek" hair dryer. The answer was that people have been inclined to file lawsuits against the hotel owners when they pick up a hair dryer that is already plugged in and then drop it in the water in the sink or bathtub and shock their dumb asses. The visceral act of finding the dryer and plugging it up removes any liability the hotel chain has for the stupidity of the litigious idiots who think it is somebody else's fault they did not get the brief or brief their kids on electricity and water somewhere in their lives. These are the same people who want to sue McDonald's for having hot coffee, feeding them fatty burgers and fries, or those who sue the maniac responsible for the emotional trauma associated with a five-mile-per-hour fender bender. If I get started on the rain maker, lottery, socialist, entitlement, income redistribution from the hard to the hardly working mentality that so many in our country have evolved to, I'll have to start another book or just shit myself in disgust.

The only other major problem with hotels is wall thickness and adjoining rooms. Some hotels are better than others with regard to soundproofing rooms. But if you end up very often in a hotel with a crappy bed, you will inevitably find one with thin walls, or adjoining doors with a two-inch gap between the bottom of the floor and the door. If more people understood the laws of physics and how sound travels, this would not be a problem, but on numerous occasions I have been blessed with the blaring of the next door neighbor's television, heard all manner of phone sex, and occasionally some real live, right there, headboard banging into my wall and shaking my bed sex. As titillating as that might sound, it is generally during the time when the solo traveler is trying to sleep. If I had wanted a vibrating bed, I'd have stayed in one of the more seedy motels around town. If you check into a room and can hear the TV in the next room, immediately ask for a new room. Some hotels are so bad you cannot escape the problem, but sometimes you might get lucky and get some peace and quiet.

On the rental car front, the government doesn't pay for the really good companies, so we are accustomed to the low-cost compact, no-frills vehicles offered by all rental agencies. I don't have any strong preferences or advice on this front, but I can tell you that if you ever find yourself in a Toyota Prius, make sure you get the brief on how to get the car started and moving. I arrived in Memphis one rainy evening and was using one of the rental car companies that allow you to pick your vehicle off the row with that class of rental. I walked out and saw an old fellow in a Prius, and the only other car in my row was a Pontiac G-6. I heard the old guy cursing. The Prius's lights were on, as were the wipers and left turn signal. The old guy sees me walking out and runs over to the Pontiac and takes off. I walked up to the Prius and the key was lying on the floor. He had no idea where it went and neither did I. As a highly skilled information technology program manager, I began to deduce how to start this vehicle. It was raining and dark and I pulled the owner's manual out of the floor. I kept looking for the one page that told you how to start the car, and it was scattered among the forty torn-out pages that had been left in the passenger floorboard. Guess the old guy had the same idea and did not like what the owner's manual had had to say about it. As I scanned the digital dashboard, I turned off the turn signal and figured out how to turn on the radio. I put my foot on the brake and moved the gear selector from park into drive. Somehow in that process the car just started. No key, no starter, and it started. Not one to mess with success, I took off. Turning the car off was a cinch, but the next day I had the same adventure when trying to figure out how to get the damn thing started. Through a series of random knob movements and foot movements, it started again and off I went. By the third day, I had figured out the mystery of starting a Prius but will not share it with you. It's too much fun to sort out on your own. And for the rental car people out there, a "Prius quick start" guide with the rental contract would be a really cool idea.

So after all of this sage counsel, if the dung beetle manager must travel, do so in the confidence that it is not the fun boondoggle most people perceive it to be. Arm yourself with the recognition and evasion techniques noted in this book, hope for the best, and expect the worst.

CHAPTER 12

CLOSING THOUGHTS

Some of you may have heard of stealth shitter stories from time to time. Stealth shitters sneak around, make a deposit somewhere in the workplace besides the local toilet, and leave the prize for some unsuspecting individual to find the next day. I have personally witnessed two such events in my career (both happened in the same organization). The first was a case of the "shit-can shitter" who would sneak into the boss's work areas and take a dump in their garbage cans. Since this particular set of bosses came in extremely early, they were able to get the suspicious deposits taken into custody before the workforce came in and heard about it or smelled something afoul. This game of cat and mouse went on for about six months and the perpetrator was never caught, nor did the issue find its way out into public information in the facility.

Many years later, there was another case in which someone would smear feces around on bathroom walls. At least this one stayed in the confines of the restroom. Unfortunately, the word did get out about the scat bathroom painter, partly due to the leadership getting on a public address system and talking about the likely mental instability of the perpetrator. This same leadership also had the enterprising idea of placing video surveillance cameras in the toilets to try and catch the "shit-smearing bandit" in the act on videotape. The cameras were not well hidden and discovered by those not shitting and smearing it on the walls, and there was a subsequent public apology and removal of the monitoring devices. This bandit also remained in the shadows and escaped prosecution. And no, it wasn't me. Shit really happens, and sometimes it happens at work by people you work with.

I'm not really sure where this book will end up if it ever makes it to a bookstore. It could be filed under business and management, humor, or the personal memoirs of a strange federal manager. It is my sincere hope that whether or not you found any diamonds among the dung pile, you at least had a good time and a few laughs while reading through this emerging management philosophy. This book has been a lifetime in the making for me and was a lot of fun to write. The strange and unusual way things weaved together to give me this "brown" view of modern management is a direct by-product of life in rural Arkansas and my experience in the low to middle tier bureaucratic suck. I am positive that it is applicable to all dung beetle managers and all members of the workforce everywhere, whether in the federal, state, or local government or local grocery store.

I have read countless management and leadership books that spend hundreds of pages droning on about profoundly obvious, simple truths. Good habits are good. Trust is good. Empowerment is good. Waste is bad. Quality is good. The economy is complex. The Internet is transformational. Leadership is hard. Change is hard. Many of these books provide great insight, but they don't really challenge you to spin your head around and think about things from a fundamentally different perspective. The modern workforce needs a new way of looking at the challenges of the 21st century. Our dung beetle friends and all of the shitters in the world provide a clear and elementary foundation to understand basic leadership and management. If nothing else, they provide some really fun labels to toss around with your colleagues to keep things light while trying to make sense of the chaos.

With the recent change of administrations and the ballooning of the federal workforce, this book is very timely for those paying taxes to fund the ever expanding bureaucracy, and those who find themselves employed by it. I'll go on record saying that expanding the federal government and government meddling with private markets is a hazardous long-term undertaking for our country. The best and worst part of our economic system is that things fail when they are not efficient. If we don't let them fail and prop them up in the name of social goodness, we cripple the necessary technological and behavioral changes that are core to market transformation in a modern capitalist economy. We simply don't have enough rollers in our economy to stave off the impending encrustation that is likely to occur when the bureaucrats get augured in and established with their pounds of checklists, policies, and regulations. The cost and innate inefficiency of government organizations will be with us and our grandchildren for a very long time.

The American system of government was not designed to be a lean, mean, responsive, and efficient machine. Speed to market at the federal level can be very dangerous when the necessary constructive tensions designed into our legislative process are not followed. Debate and facts can be overwhelmed by demagoguery and emotion, and we can end up with unchecked streams of federal spending that are not managed well or laws and policies that cripple the future of the nation. There is no one right answer in a democracy, but a prevailing belief in what is right or wrong based on the circumstances and verifiable facts at a given time. So we fight every day to separate the shit from the shinola in the circumstances and seek the indisputable facts to make our decisions. And that is where this book comes in, as a tool you can use to put a different lens on the problem, or to simply make you pause, relax, and have a good laugh while working it out.

Many of us go through life believing that we alone cannot make much of a difference in the world. I use the analogy that some people view their life like farting while zooming down the road at 60 MPH on a big ass Harley – it may feel good and score a 9.8 on the geez scale, but who's going to notice? It's all about perspective. Looking down at the earth from the moon, we are individually indistinguishable from the one big blue ball. Looking up at the moon from the earth, it looks like one big silver ball. The rest of the planets, the stars, and sun all look like balls. Let's face it: we're surrounded by a universe of dung balls. It is no wonder the Egyptians thought so highly of the dung beetle.

Fat starts one cell at a time. Cancer starts one cell at a time. Health starts one cell at a time. The big blue ball we live on makes it through each day one living organism at a time. You make your life one decision at a time. Somewhere in the past that has no beginning point and in the future that has no end, individual cellular and organism actions formed the world we have today and will define the one that will exist long after each of us have made our deposits, fecal or other, on the planet and cosmos. This celestial dung ball we call Earth is ours to shit on, roll, tunnel in, and dwell in. So if this "life on Earth" thing is going to work out well, we all need each other doing what we do every day to the best of our ability while keeping the rest of us in mind. Shit really does happen, it always will, and it really has to be cleaned up.

The next time you happen to go by a pasture, take a moment and imagine what would happen without the dung beetle continuously tearing down the dung pats, aerating the soil, and ensuring a disease-free source of food for the cow. Then go home and remember to thank the dung beetles when you enjoy the milk, hamburger, and steaks. The econometrician in me would love to have provided you with all manner of graphs and statistics to prove or disprove my points, but sometimes things just make common sense and you don't have to have a PhD to observe the obvious. To all of you dung beetle managers out there, keep diving in, rolling on, and looking behind you from time to time. Yours stinks too.

LaVergne, TN USA
04 November 2009

162962LV00001B/1/P